Maximum Dream Achievement

How You Can Live and Enjoy a Purpose-Full Life

By
Kenn Renner and Eddie Smith

ISBN-13 978-1481850476
ISBN-10 1481850474

Copyright © 2013 by Kenn Renner and Eddie Smith
Printed in the United States of America

No part of this publication may be reproduced, stored in a retrieval system, or transmitted in any form by any means – electronic, mechanical, digital photocopy, recording, or any other without the prior permission of the authors.

All rights reserved solely by the authors. The authors guarantee all contents are original and do not infringe upon the legal rights of any other person or work. No part of this book may be reproduced without the permission of the authors. The views expressed in this book are not necessarily those of the publisher.

Morissa Schwartz, line editor
Daniel Sanford, cover and layout design

Endorsements

"It's no secret that many motivational books and material today are filled with new age mysticism. I am delighted to see Kenn Renner, one of America's top realtors, and Eddie Smith, noted Christian author and conference speaker, present us with a biblically-based approach to the proven success process of goal setting to achieve those dreams that God has placed within us."

Dr. Pat Robertson
CEO, Christian Broadcasting Network
Virginia Beach, Virginia

"Every truly successful person will tell you that they began their journey to success by setting goals. This book is full of the building blocks you'll use to construct yourself a beautiful life."

Tom Hopkins
Best-selling author and world's leading authority on selling, author of *How to Master the Art of Selling*

"The most important thing you can know is that your sins are forgiven and heaven is your home. Another important thing for you to know is your God-given earthly assignment. *Maximum Dream Achievement* by my long-time friend Eddie Smith and Kenn Renner offers direction on how we can recognize the dreams God has placed in our hearts and position ourselves to reach them."

Arthur Blessitt
Minister, Author, Evangelist
Guinness World Record Holder (World's Longest Walk)

"*Maximum Dream Achievement* is a must read for all who truly want the most fulfilled life possible! It's a great combination

www.MaximumDreamAchievement.com

of thought provoking message with actionable techniques to move your forward. Purpose-FULL to say the least!"

Scott Schilling
Best Selling Author, Speaker, Trainer and Coach

"If you are ready to discover what you really want and how to step into your destiny this book will serve as your blueprint. This far more than a "how-to" book. It will lift your spirit and inspire your soul. Don't miss Appendix A. The wisdom and information there is worth the whole book."

Dr. Rick C. Ernst
Author of Richer Life Secrets
TheBestCoach.com

"In his book *Eat that Frog* Brian Tracy writes, 'Goals are the fuel in the furnace of achievement.' We motivational speakers continually urge those who would achieve, to set goals and take strategic steps to reach them.

Now my friends Kenn Renner and Eddie Smith have combined their considerable experience and abilities to give us *Maximum Dream Achievement*, a step-by-step easy-to-follow guide to reaching our goals. I encourage you to dig in. You might well find your future and your fortune within these pages."

Daniel Hall
Author, speaker and marketing consultant
www.DanielHallPresents.com

"Kenn and Eddie have brought a holistic approach to reaching your goals by incorporating mind and soul into what others have only listed as 'to-dos.' This clear and direct manual reads much like a motivational book, leaving you inspired to achieve your dreams and equipped with the tools to actually do it!"

Danny Thompson
Director of Publishing
Keller Williams International

"If you need clarity and inspiration to achieve the boldest goals, Kenn and Eddie's book will provide you with a path to a place most people will never dare to visit."

Ben Kinney
Vice President, Keller Williams Technology

"Kenn Renner and Eddie Smith have an incredible 12-point approach to goal setting that exceeds anything I've ever seen. It taps the emotional, visionary nerves as well as the practical step-by-step procedure. You will achieve or supersede your goals with their formula. I read anything Kenn and Eddie write!"

Scott Carley
Motivational Speaker and Coach

www.MaximumDreamAchievement.com

Table of Contents

Endorsements	i
Table of Contents	iv
Introductions	vi
Foreword	xii

Chapter 1: Introduction to Goal Setting — 1

Chapter 2: Step One – Want — 11
Want / Desire / Decide / Commit

Chapter 3: Step Two – Know — 21
Know / Believe / Faith

Chapter 4: Step Three – Ink — 31
Write It / Speak It / Proclaim It

Chapter 5: Step Four – Motives — 39
List Benefits / List Consequences / Motivations

Chapter 6: Step Five – Boundaries — 45
Analyze Starting Point / Define Completion / Boundaries

Chapter 7: Step Six – Time — 53
Set a Deadline / Set a Starting Date / The Stopwatch

Chapter 8: Step Seven – Survey — 57
List Obstacles / Identify Opportunities / Survey Territory

Chapter 9: Step Eight – Information — 67
Identify Information / List Resources / Research

www.MaximumDreamAchievement.com

Chapter 10: Step Nine – Advocates   73
Identify Those Helpers / Identify Those to Avoid / Advocacy

Chapter 11 – Step Ten – Plan   81
Make a Plan / Take Action / Activation

Chapter 12 – Step Eleven – Consume   91
Visualize / Emotionalize / Internalize

Chapter 13 – Step Twelve – Power   101
Persistence / Patience / Prayer

Action Exercises   115

Appendix A   135

Introduction
Kenn Renner. Co-author

It was many years ago, in the mid-1980s, when late one night an all too familiar voice came on the television. It was motivational specialist Tony Robbins. He said that he had once lived in a one-bedroom apartment in Venice, California where he got fed up with his life, which seemed to be going nowhere. That day he decided he would take massive action to change his circumstances. He concluded that since others had come from humble beginnings and achieved great things by changing their thinking and setting goals, then he could too.

As I listened to Tony I realized that I was also a kid in a one-bedroom apartment who felt like things weren't going my way. That night, I too decided to take massive action. I would learn and model what others had done to achieve great things.

I began attending seminars, reading books, and listening to audio programs. I wrote down goals and made plans of action. Gradually my life began to turn around. I moved from living on credit cards to starting businesses and prospering. Success didn't happen overnight—it was the journey that was fulfilling.

When God created the first man, Adam, He commanded him to "be fruitful and multiply." God's not into mere addition. He's into multiplication! Jesus told us that we were to "bear much fruit." Life is seasonal. There are times to sow and there are times to reap. At times we all feel that we are not bearing much of anything—that we are falling short of the mark. Rest assured that once you begin to write down your goals and take purposeful action each day to achieve them (sowing), things will change. You will live (reap) the fruit-filled life you were put on Earth to live.

Maximum Dream Achievement

Living a purposeful life is about moving step-by-step toward a prosperous and fulfilling life. This book is based on a book that I wrote called *Power Goals: Twelve Proven Steps to Make Your Dreams Come True* in which I offer readers scriptural wisdom to help them move from where they are to where they want to be. The biblical references were veiled (hidden) so the book would not become pigeon holed as a "Christian" work. I wrote it for a secular audience and didn't want to sound "preachy." But truth be told, the ancient wisdom of God's Word saturates that book. Before I wrote *Power Goals*, I knew that there would be two versions: one targeted for a secular audience; and another version for believers (or soon to be believers).

Then I met my friend and mentor Eddie Smith from Houston, Texas. Eddie and his wonderful wife Alice (both bestselling Christian authors) have a passion to help people around the world come to faith in Jesus Christ and grow as Christians. We agreed that one thing which seemed to be missing in the church today was teaching on setting and achieving goals. In fact, there seems to be a common belief that if we simply "live by faith," God will take care of the rest.

Clearly we must live by faith. But we are clearly directed to exercise good stewardship of ourselves and our possessions. We are to discover the dreams that God has placed in our hearts and take purposeful action to position ourselves to see them fulfilled. His Word states that "faith without works is dead." Eddie agreed to infuse practical biblical commentary and wisdom into this new book that we call *Maximum Dream Achievement*. Eddie's input shows how we Christians are to find God's purpose for our lives, set attainable goals, and make strategic plans for their achievement.

For over 50 years, Eddie has travelled the world equipping Christian and non-Christian leaders alike. The list of people he has counseled and prayed with is a virtual "who's-who" of some of the most powerful and influential movers and shakers of our time. It is a huge honor for me to have him as co-author of this book. But it did not come as a surprise.

Why? Many years ago I wrote down a goal to "co-author a book with a bestselling author." Surprise, surprise—God makes things happen when we exercise faith, write out what we'd like to see come to pass, and take purposeful action! That is what this book is about. It's to show you how you can partner with God to do the things and achieve the dreams that He put you on Earth to do. God wants you to live a happy, healthy, and prosperous life, which is also my prayer for you.

See you at the top!

Kenn Renner
Entrepreneur/Speaker/Author

Introduction
Eddie Smith, Co-author

I was the youngest Fidelity Union Life insurance agent at the tender age of 19 years. My general agent (trainer/manager) was a kind and godly man. As my first success coach, he took me under his wing and began to enlarge my view of success in life. At his recommendation, I began to read everything I could find about success. Some of my early inspirations were the writings of the late and legendary Charlie "Tremendous" Jones. Another was the pioneer of success, world-changer, Zig Ziglar who recently went to be with the Lord. Little did I dream that I would one day know these two men personally.

Men like Charlie and Zig, each a strong outspoken Christian, have spent their lives teaching others how to set and achieve their goals. It's in their tradition that my friend and co-author, Kenn Renner, and I offer this book to help you achieve your dreams. We not only believe that God puts dreams in the hearts of His children; but that He enables them to achieve them. Unfortunately, many of us fail to identify our dreams as "God deposits" in our hearts, and we dismiss them as simply our wild fantasies.

After more than fifty years of ministry I assure you that God wants only the best for you. The dreams He has placed in your heart won't be things you will dread at all. They will delight you! After all, they are expressions of your loving heavenly Father.

For *Maximum Dream Achievement* you should know that God not only gives you the dreams, He will also equip you to achieve them. How does He do that? It all begins with receiving Jesus Christ as your Lord and Savior. After all, He is "the Way, the Truth, and the Life." Christ came that we might

www.MaximumDreamAchievement.com

have abundant life. He wants us to live and enjoy purpose-FULL lives! True life begins with Christ! That's foundational.

However, there is more. In this book, we provide the steps that if taken will position you to realize your fullest potential. The favor of God is real. However, if we aren't in position to receive and enjoy it, we'll miss the benefits.

I pray that our book will bless and benefit you. Be sure to share your success stories with us.

Maximum Blessings!

Eddie Smith
Bestselling Author, Speaker, Marketing, and Writing Coach

www.MaximumDreamAchievement.com

Foreword

When one peruses the New York Times Best Seller List week after week, motivational and how to books always top the list. We all want to achieve our life dreams. We all want to find the keys to personal success and achievement. And it's true, we have read books that were little more than pomp and idealism; nothing but fantasy. Too often these books are filled with grand ideas that are unrealistic or impractical. They may make great content for a science fiction novel, but they don't work in the real world of hard work and vision planning. So while exciting to read, nothing much materializes.

I am glad to write that this isn't so with *Maximum Dream Achievement*. I couldn't put Kenn and Eddie's book down! Each chapter delivers practical insight on how to set realistic reachable goals, and maintain a positive attitude. The exercises and time charts they offer will help you monitor your success.

Many men and women today lack personal character, which disqualifies their message. Kenn and Eddie are both men of moral character. While only fools will take the advice of someone without integrity, I assure you that Eddie and Kenn live what they write.

As a best-selling author and co-author of over 15 books, I assure you that the key to readability is to offer a product with which a reader can identify. *Maximum Dream Achievement* is such a book! I couldn't put the book down until I had read every page. Not only did it encourage me, but I felt energized and ready to set goals for current and future projects. Don't overlook this great opportunity to be changed….you can thank me later.

Dr. Alice Smith
U.S. Prayer Center, Houston, TX

www.MaximumDreamAchievement.com

Chapter 1
Introduction to Goal Setting

Goal Setting

Goal setting has proven to be the single most powerful way for one to achieve desired results. More success has been attributed to goal setting than to any other method or strategy. Throughout history, those who have learned to set goals and to take purposeful action towards achieving them have accomplished their objectives and changed the world.

Today, more than ever, learning to set goals will to a large degree determine our ultimate success. Less than three percent of the world's population has written goals. More than eighty percent of the world's wealth is controlled by less than three percent of its population. Is there a correlation between the three percent who have written goals and the majority of wealth being controlled by such a small minority? There most assuredly is.

> **A goal is a crystalized view of that which is possible.**

What is a goal? A goal is a crystalized view of that which is possible; a written expression of one's intention that is tied to one's purpose. God has created each of us on purpose and for a purpose. An understanding of our purpose and a deep commitment to it, accompanied by clearly defined written goals, will propel us toward accomplishing our purpose—which is ultimate success!

Compellingly written, targeted, purpose-based goals will guide us to our God-given destinies like a roadmap and compass. With written goals we are able to take appropriate action and can move forward toward reaching our kingdom potential.

King Solomon, one of the richest and wisest men in history wrote, *"Where there is no vision the people perish..."* (Prov 29:18a, KJV). Contrarily we could say that where there *is* a vision the people *flourish*.

People, companies, churches and nations suffer when there is a lack of direction and vision or goals. On the other hand, they prosper in an atmosphere with established goals and appropriate action plans. Those of us with big goals will lead the way toward big results.

If written goals are this vital to success, then why do so few people have them?

One reason that so few people set goals is that they were never taught to do so. You can have the equivalent of a university degree (16-18 years of formal education) and not have had one hour of instruction on goal setting. That's a shame. One of our goals as we write this book is to help change that. Goal setting can be learned, and it can become a lifelong habit.

Another reason people don't set goals is because of their fear of failure. They assume that if they set goals and fail to achieve them, they will let themselves or others down. Apparently they don't realize that their failure to set goals and work to achieve them will absolutely lead to disappointment. However, rather than facing the pain of failure, they don't set even simple goals, much less lofty ones. It's a common problem. One thing is certain. That notion isn't from God. God isn't the source of fear. You may recall that the Apostle Paul told his young mentee Timothy, *"...God hath not given us a spirit of fear; but of power, and of love, and of a sound mind"* (2 Timothy 1:7).

Some people don't set goals, because they aren't certain what it is that they really want. Remember, everyone was born for a purpose. We all need to determine what our purpose is and what we are created to accomplish. Until we know what we are here to achieve, we won't have a target to hit. No archer pulls back an arrow in his bow without first taking time to identify a target.

First, determine the purpose for which you were created. Second, know what it is that you want. Then go for it. There is an ancient Greek aphorism that exhorts us, "know thyself." For we who are Christians, knowing our identity in Christ is foundational to "knowing ourselves." To know our individual motivational gifts (Romans 12:3-8) is also crucial to our success.

> **Most success stories are a series of trials and errors.**

Most success stories are a series of trials and errors. Our errors are only true failures if we don't learn from them.

We see that quite clearly in the life of Simon Peter in the Bible. Although Peter went as far as to deny Christ three times near the time of Christ's crucifixion, he would later become a primary leader of the Church, and one of those who helped pen the Bible!

One of the keys to goal achievement is persistence--*a never give up attitude*. We must keep the end result in mind and never stop working toward it. Add to that the practice of patience, and we'll cross the finish line with perfect timing.

Although some success stories sound as if the paths were easy, the reality is that the paths to success are littered with setbacks. The setbacks along the way didn't mean that the individuals themselves were failures. The only ones who truly fail are those who don't learn from their experience, and those who give up and quit. Those are the ones who short-circuit their dreams and never see them come to fruition.

Face it…setbacks are inevitable. Like the title of John Maxwell's book suggests, one must learn to *Fail Forward*. Past failures don't ensure future ones. Let's consider our setbacks as "educational experiences." Then set new goals and start on new journeys.

We have a saying in our (Kenn's) family—"Winning is everything." At first, it was meant to be a joke. But the more I thought about it the more I realized the truth it contains. We must all maintain a winning attitude. We must want to win. After all, losing is the only alternative to winning!

To miss a winning shot or come up short in a relay race doesn't make one "a loser." Winners are winners even when they suffer setbacks. Failure and recovery along the way is also part of winning. As a the Apostle Paul once said, *"one thing I do – forgetting what is behind and straining towards what is ahead, I press on towards the goal to win the prize"* (Philippians 3:13-14). Winning begins as an attitude; then over time it becomes a lifestyle.

Standard Setting

If goal setting seems a bit overwhelming at first, we suggest that you start with "standard setting." Your standards are the personal boundaries that you establish. Each of us has standards for ourselves and for our businesses. However, some of us may have never taken the time to identify and to evaluate our standards. For example, you most likely have standards for your income, standards for your health, and for your weight. Standards are "goals in disguise." Our minimum standards change our perspective of what we expect of ourselves.

The word *standard* means to "stand hard." In military terms, a *standard* is a flag or banner that is raised to indicate a solid position or stance of an armed force. We call the one who carries that flag, "the standard bearer." Whether we know it or not, we all have standards. If we don't set our own standards, others will do it for us. The consequences of falling below our minimum standards can be disappointment and even pain.

At one time, I (Kenn) felt that a personal income of $5,000 per month was a lofty goal. When I achieved that goal I had a huge sense of accomplishment and rightly so. However, $5,000 per month would be below my minimum standard today. It would mean a drastic reduction in my lifestyle. Five figures per month would be my minimum standard, and my goal is much higher than that. What was once a lofty goal is now well below my current standard. To my amazement, my business endeavors provide a standard income of more than five figures each month. My goal: earn six or even seven figures per month.

When asked why he sets such high goals, a man replied, "I'd rather shoot for the stars and miss them, than shoot for nothing and hit it."

We encourage you to establish your minimum standards. Go ahead and write them out. Follow them with your "reach for the stars goals." As you increase your minimum income standard incrementally you create stepping-stones toward reaching your greater goals. So set your initial standards and then systematically raise them. Soon, what once seemed like lofty goals will become your minimum standard—your new norm.

100% Responsibility

An underlying key to success is to realize that each of us is *100% responsible* for the decisions that we make. Although we are not responsible for all the difficulties and trials that we encounter along the way, we are responsible for our responses to them.

> **Each of us is ultimately responsible for him or herself.**

Two common "diseases" that work against success are *blame* and *entitlement*. Far too many people blame others or their circumstances for their failures. Some actually expect the government to take care of them. Refusing to work, they assume that they are entitled to government handouts. The bottom line is this. Each of us is ultimately responsible for him or herself.

Along with *blame* and *entitlement,* we often find a third debilitating disease—*excuses*. Aren't you tired of hearing excuses? We are. Frankly, there is no excuse for excuses. Yet we have all heard or have been heard to say, "It's not my fault." At one time or another we've all used excuses to justify why we didn't or could not do something that was expected of us. Let's determine today to abandon excuse-making in the future.

If we're to achieve success in life, we must take responsibility for ourselves, humbly rejoice in our successes, graciously admit to our failures, and realize that the power to choose is ours. We can either determine to boldly step into our preferred future or to cower back to a life of mediocrity. We've chosen the abundant life!

Perhaps you're unfamiliar with the term *abundant life*. It was Jesus who announced in John 10:10 that He had come to bring *life* to humankind—*abundant life!* I (Eddie) have imagined what those who heard Him say that must have thought. They certainly would have considered themselves fully alive. After all, they had blood flowing in their veins. They must have wondered what He could possibly have meant.

The truth is, they were alive, but not yet "fully alive." Why so? To be fully alive one must receive Christ, because

Christ Himself IS life—abundant and eternal. John wrote it this way in 1 John 5:12, *"He who has the Son (Jesus), has life."*

I (Eddie) was in a meeting of Christian psychologists and pastoral counselors when one of them explained with a smile, "We no longer refer to our clients as *victims*. We call them *survivors*."

At that I responded, "Survivors? Why don't you call them what God calls them—*more than conquerors* and *overcomers?* (Romans 8:37; 1 John 4:4)

Go ahead—join us! Decide that you are not going to be a victim and make the choice to become a victor.

Are You Ready to Become a "Three Percenter?"

According to achievement expert Brian Tracy only three percent of the population has written goals. We challenge you to become a member of *The Three Percent Club*: the three percent of people who have written down their clearly defined, inspiring, lofty goals and their constantly increasing minimum standards.

> **...only three percent of the population has written goals.**

Once you join *The Three Percent Club*, by writing down your goals, you too will begin to experience supernatural results; and enjoy the incredible power of goal setting. You'll begin to accomplish infinitely more than you think.

God favors abundance. As we've pointed out, He said to Adam and Eve in Genesis 1:28, *"Be fruitful and multiply."* He calls the Christ-life we are to live, *the abundant life*. I (Eddie) write quite a bit about this in my book, *How to Be Heard in Heaven* (Available at http://PrayerBookstore.com). In it, I suggest that God doesn't merely want to answer our prayers. He wants to give us *"...exceedingly, abundantly above all that we can ask* (pray) *or imagine* (think)" (Ephesians 3:20). I point out that one of my favorite prayers, based on that truth, is "Lord, surprise me."

The good news about goal setting is it is a *learned activity*. Virtually anyone can do it, will you? I (Kenn) was taught goal setting many years ago by an audio program that changed my life.

Since then it has been reinforced by seminars I've attended and books I've read. I have learned goal setting and achievement from teachers like Jim Rohn, Brian Tracy, Tony Robbins, Jack Canfield, Zig Ziglar, Napoleon Hill, Myles Monroe, the Bible, and others. I learned it, I do it today, and I teach others to do it. It's a habit well worth forming and is a lifelong exercise that produces incredible results.

The Twelve Steps

The 12-step goal setting technique that we share with you in this book will work for your small and your big goals. It will even work for your "B-HAGs" (your Big Hairy Audacious Goals). This 12-step strategy will work for both your personal and your business goals. It is effective in the physical, mental, as well as the spiritual realms. The 12-steps may seem at first like a lot of work. However, when you make them a habit they can be done in as little as ten to fifteen minutes.

Our 12-steps strategy is adapted from Brian Tracy's classic audio program *Maximum Achievement*. After years of using this method, we feel that the clarification we offer in this book makes Tracy's program even more effective. We've broken each of the 12 steps into three components that will greatly enhance the experience and effectiveness of your goal setting exercise.

Goals Journal

Most of the great achievement experts encourage the use of a "goals journal." A goals journal provides a central place in which to keep one's written dreams and goals. I (Kenn) have kept goals journals for decades. It's inspiring for me to look back in my goals journals and see thoughts and dreams I had years ago.

A goals journal will help you track your progress. It is both a place to record great ideas, and it will become a source of inspiration. We strongly encourage you to keep a goals journal for all of your plans and projects.

At the conclusion of this book you'll find action exercises, and a place to keep your personal notes and resolutions. You can start your journal with these pages if you like. Or you can purchase a journal in which to record your dreams and goals at your local office supply store. Follow through with each action exercise in this book. They are for your benefit to help you create your preferred future.

I (Eddie) would remind you that the Old Testament prophet Habakkuk knew the importance of this principle. It was He who wrote, *"Write the vision; make it plain on tablets, so he may run who reads it"* (Habakkuk 2:2, ESV).

If you are a leader, for you to have goals and know them personally is important, but it's insufficient. You should write them clearly and publish them prominently. Post them on your organization's bulletin boards. Mention them in the monthly newsletter. Be creative. The problem with many businesses, churches and other nonprofits is that even if the leader has a vision and written goals, the staff and members either don't know them or can't succinctly explain them.

In our next chapter we will embark on the journey 12 steps toward learning how to achieve our goals, dreams, and aspirations.

Chapter 2
Step One - Want

Desire / Decide / Commit

"What do you want?"
— Jesus (John 1:38)

One day, as Jesus passed John the Baptist and two of his disciples, John shouted, *"Behold the Lamb of God!"* Upon hearing that, John's two disciples began to follow Jesus. At that, Jesus turned to them and asked, *"What do you want?"* (From John 1:34-38). It's a simple question, but quite profound. The truth is, too many people have yet to determine what they want out of life. They virtually watch their life pass by day-after-day without any sense of direction at all.

As we begin this journey together our question for you is, "What do you really want?" Think about it. If you could have anything that your heart desires today, what would it be?

I (Eddie) have met some believers who shy away from the idea of goal setting. They'd point out that Psalm 37:23 states that *"the steps of a good man are ordered by the LORD."* Therefore, setting goals is unnecessary. And Proverbs 3:6 tells us, *"In all thy ways acknowledge him, and he shall direct thy paths."* Believing it holy to do so, they sit passively waiting for things to happen. They feel it would be "unspiritual" to dream, to set goals, or to take the initiative.

Around 3,000 years ago King David, the psalmist, revealed an incredible promise from God when he wrote: *"Delight yourself in the LORD, and he will give you the desires of your heart"* (Psalm 37:4, ESV). Do you see it? With Christ at the center of our lives, His will means more to us than our own. Our thoughts, feelings, and decisions begin to align with His. We will find ourselves wanting for ourselves what He wants for us.

Can we miss it? Certainly we can—and we will at times. But when we approach it from the standpoint of our being one with Him and His being our Lord, we will become sensitive to His "redirection" in our lives. We see that demonstrated as Jesus prayed in the garden when facing His crucifixion, *"Not my will, but yours be done"* (Luke 22:42). He submitted His will to His Father's. We've both seen God reshape and redirect our dreams (goals).

So go ahead and dream. Dream big! When you walk with Him, you'll discover that He will plant His dreams along with yours in your heart! In fact, Jesus told His followers,

"...he will himself be able to do the things I do; and he will do even greater things than these" (John 14:12). Wow! With Christ you are destined to do great things!

Desire

For a goal to come to fruition, it should be something we truly want. We must not just casually *want it*. We must intensely passionately *desire it*! The biggest achievements are realized because of one's intense burning desire, and a "no quit" attitude.

When Bill Gates of *Microsoft Corporation* proclaimed that he wanted his product on "every desk in the world" his was no casual desire. It was his passion and drive that eventually enabled him to overcome the inevitable obstacles that he encountered. Today we find his products on nearly every desk in the world.

> **Desire means "of the father."**

The word *sire* is defined as "the male parent of a quadruped." For example, a horse sires (fathers) a colt. The prefix *de* means "of." So, the word *desire* means "of the father." God, our heavenly Father, has created us with built-in dreams and desires waiting to be revealed. Like seeds He has planted in the good soil of our lives, they are waiting to burst forth with life in God's time. Not all, of course, but much of what may have seemed to us as little more than our ideas or intuition are divine seeds waiting to bear fruit in our lives.

The Father is the key to it all. When we realize this, surrender to His creative plan for our lives, and *delight* in Him, as the Psalmist said, *"He will give us the desires* (secret petitions) *of our hearts."*

A goal starts as a small strand of un-manifested "Mental DNA" in the mind of our Creator that He deposits in us where it begins its journey. The trouble is that some people don't have a clue what their purpose is. Because of this, they set purposeless goals unrelated to who God created them to be.

Our life-purpose will come into focus as we discover Him and begin to realize who He is, the gifts and abilities He has given us, and the culture in which He has planted us. As we do, our goals (and the steps to accomplish our purpose) will be clarified.

As we fervently and intensely desire to see this completed, we will begin to see results almost immediately; much more so than for us to merely wish for things. Our minds work best when we focus on precise instructions.

> **Everything to God is present tense.**

In John 5:19, Jesus explained how He only did what He saw the Father doing. We are to do the same. What is the Father doing? He is extending His kingdom and exalting His name. Those should be our overriding purposes as well. Why? We are joint venturing with God (our Father) in the family business! Congruency with our Creator is perhaps the most powerful and most overlooked aspect of success in life! As we accept this role, we will be infinitely more satisfied with the result.

Who is God? God identified Himself to Moses as "the I AM." God isn't "the I was" or "the I will be." As "the I am," He is the ever-present tense God.

That one point unlocks so much of the truth of the New Testament. Though we are bound by time and space, God isn't. *Everything to Him is present tense.*

This explains why Jesus taught that when we pray we should ask as if we <u>already have</u> that for which we are asking!

(Mark 11:24) The Apostle, Paul, came along in Philippians 4:6 and suggested that we are not to worry, but instead, we're pray with thanksgiving about everything! That's how one would pray, as Jesus pointed out, if he already had that for which he is asking. Right?

So we don't thank God for what He *will do* in the future. We thank Him for what He *is doing* in the present, even if it's yet unseen! *That's faith!* "So how does this relate to goal setting," you ask? Simply this.

When you write your goals, always write them in the *present tense.* Then add a future deadline using *present tense.* For example: "I am making $20,000 per month by June 30th," or, "I weigh __X__ pounds by December 31st."

Never forget—a goal attained is a step toward a purpose fulfilled. There are no accidents with God. He created each of us on purpose, with purpose, and purposefulness. We were designed and placed here to fulfill our desires, to solve problems; to perpetuate and to live, love, and grow in those.

Right now, what do you passionately desire? Ask yourself—*what do I really, really want?* What do you want for your family, your relationships, and for your business? What do you want for your health, your mind, your body, and your spirit? What do you want with all of your heart? Record those things in writing. At the end of this section, we'll ask you to brainstorm all the things you want without concern for limitations.

Decide

"Deciding is Igniting"

There is little responsibility in desiring. However, deciding carries great responsibility. A desire is *a wish*; but a decision is *a choice*. Wishes are modestly powerful. Choices are infinitely more powerful! Choices direct where we will end up.

You may want something, but until you decide and take action it will remain a mere desire. The word *decide* comes from a root word meaning "to cut off." Once we decide to go for that which we passionately desire, we cut off any form of retreat. We burn our bridges to alternatives behind us.

Unlike a desire, a decision is a turning point—a point of ignition. Consider this. Once the boosters of NASA's Saturn 5 rockets were fired, there was no turning back. The only alternative that remained was to reach orbit.

> **Where we will be tomorrow is being determined by the minute-by-minute, hour-by-hour, day-to-day decisions that we make.**

Our desires are important, but our decisions determine our destiny. It is our decisions that move us toward our destination! In fact, where and who we are today is a direct result of our past decisions; and where we will be tomorrow is being determined by the minute-by-minute, hour-by-hour, decisions we make today.

Did you know that each of us makes thousands of decisions daily? Some of these are consciously made, but the majority of them are made unconsciously. Every conscious decision we make is either a "yes" or a "no." "Yes, I will go that way" or "No, I will go another way."

With a set of clearly written goals our decisions will automatically gravitate toward the "right way"—the destiny we want. Clearly defined well-written goals will guide us unconsciously to remain "on track."

On the other hand, without written goals, our minds will wander. We'll soon lose focus, drift with the current, and become subject to other people's goals and objectives rather than our own. This is why the three percent of those who have written goals control eighty percent of the world's wealth. In fact, because of the level of confidence that their written goals provide, others will line up and march behind them.

Let's dream the dreams, and set the goals that will have the most positive impact on our lives—those that God has built into our DNA. Let's identify and say "no" to any desire that doesn't line up with God's created purpose for our lives.

Commit

"Commit then never quit."

We may desire something, set a goal to achieve it, and even decide to for it. But what seals the deal, is when we commit to it. In aviation, there is a point on a runway where a pilot must "commit to take off." There is no turning back. To commit is "to deliberately carry out an action." It's is a binding commitment to obligate ourselves. One might say that it is a covenant we make with ourselves—a binding covenant that's not to be broken.

I (Kenn) credit the "commit" portion of this narrative to a gentleman who came to one of my seminars. He had just sold a printing company which netted his partners and him $40 million dollars. He had recently gone to work at our local real estate office, not because he needed the money, but simply because he was fascinated by the real estate business. He explained to me that there are plenty of unsuccessful people who have specific desires, set goals to reach them, and even decide it is what they want; but they never *commit* to reaching it. They abort the launch!

| Commit in writing! |

He told me how when his company met upon hard times, was up against a wall almost to the point of bankruptcy, his partners and he tenaciously committed to pull it through. Refusing to quit, they eventually made a fortune. As with the other parts of this inspirational goal setting process, it's important that we *record our commitment in writing.*

Remember, our commitment rules out any alternative plan other than to successfully reach our goals. When I think of commitment I think of marriage or parenthood. I am fully committed to my wife and kids. I would gladly take a bullet for them. I will never give up on them. For me, marriage and parenting are life-long commitments.

Distractions, objections and conflicts will always appear to challenge us—to push us off the path. We must remain committed. We must give our goals the respect that we would give to a close family member. In fact, we've heard some people refer to their dream as their "baby." A dream worth living for is a goal worth fighting for; and yes, we may have to take a few bullets along the way.

Our great and free nation, the United States of America, was formed by the commitment of our forefathers. Their commitment to their dream provides us with the free nation that we enjoy today. Bullets did fly, and through the years many have paid the ultimate price. Theirs was an example of *total commitment.*

They didn't say, "It would be kind of nice to have a free nation for our children's children, but if it doesn't work out, that's okay?" Instead, they resolved to make and to keep America free. As the saying goes, "freedom isn't free."

Goal achievement isn't free either. We must commit in advance to pay the price necessary to reach our dream. A goal without a commitment has no power. We challenge you to resolve today to commit to reaching your goals. Make a do or die choice to see your dreams become reality.

At the end of each chapter, you will be referred to an Action Exercise near the end of this book. These action exercises will greatly enhance the effectiveness of your goal setting journey. These exercises are extremely important, so please don't skip them. You can start your goals journal with these exercises. You will find a downloadable version of these Action Exercises at www.MaximumDreamAchievement.com. We encourage you to print them out.

Now complete the Action Exercise for Step One on page 115.

www.MaximumDreamAchievement.com

Chapter 3
Step Two – Know

Believe / Faith / Know

Believe

"...Everything is possible for one who believes"
Jesus (Mark 9:23b)

Belief is a powerful force that has shaped cultures, religions, and nations. Our beliefs are closely tied to our values—what we believe to be important and worthy, and what isn't. What do you believe? What are your core values? For what causes do you stand? The goals that we set, and expect to reach, must line up with (be congruent with) our core values.

Pick five of your core values, or things that you deem important. Take a moment and write them down. Now make sure the goals that you set are congruent with these core values. We won't work hard for something we don't value. Our core values are the foundation of all that we do. Our beliefs are the framework that provides the structure of our current reality and will provide support for our future reality.

Each of us has a worldview. We filter our view of the world through our beliefs, which to a large part form "our reality"—*what we believe is real to us*. Although truth is absolute, what we believe to be true is "our reality." As automobile mogul Henry Ford said: "Whether you believe you can do a thing or not, you are right."

Here's the secret. When we believe our goals are achievable our minds go to work to figure out "how." We call this our *mindset*.

No matter how big our dream is we must first believe that it's attainable. The word *believe* means, "to allow." When we truly believe we can reach our goals, we allow them to be fulfilled. Jesus Christ said in Mark 9:23b, *"…all things are possible for one who believes."* Belief (faith) is to consciously receive in advance that to which one is committed.

Faith it until we make it.

The author of the Book of Hebrews wrote: *"Now faith is being sure of what we hope for and certain of what we do not see"* (Hebrews 11:1). We should say to ourselves, "I believe I will do this, I *believe* this is for me." Perhaps you're familiar with the old adage that says that we must *"fake* it until we make it." *We don't support "faking" anything*. It's better that we *"faith* it until we make it."

The moment we believe we can accomplish a thing; we are well on our way to achieving it. When we believe that God will provide what we need; we are well on our way to receiving it. Wouldn't it be a shame for us to get to heaven and discover a storeroom that contained everything that we needed here while on Earth, but forfeited it due to our unbelief?

To believe means to mentally agree and accept a thing to be true. When we believe in a cause, we *agree with* and *accept* what it stands for. For a goal to become a reality we must believe to our core that it is meant for us, to accept it as *ours*, and to own the rights to it. Our beliefs mold our stream of thought and shape our decisions. From time to time we all need some R&R—that is to *review* and to *renew* our beliefs. Romans 12:2 admonishes us to "be transformed by renewing our minds."

> **Each of us needs to review and to renew our beliefs at times.**

Regardless of who we are, we need to *monitor* our thinking lest faulty beliefs creep back into our conscious thinking. When they do, we recognize them and remove them. Faulty beliefs like, "I can't;" "I'm not worthy;" "I'm too old;" or "I'm too young." Such thoughts will sabotage our success. We are largely the result of who we believe we can be. Similarly, we do what we believe we can do, and we have what we believe we can have.

Goal setting times are perfect times for us to reflect and sort through our thought patterns to see which of them are based on our belief system. That's when we can identify our conclusions that strengthen our resolve and those that weaken it. Once we've identified those self-defeating beliefs, we should cast them off and adopt new invigorating ones.

> **We aren't responsible for our thoughts, but we are responsible for our thinking.**

Are you familiar with the term "GIGO?" To those in the fields of computer science and information technology, GIGO is an acronym for "garbage in, garbage out." I (Eddie) often say, "We aren't responsible for our thoughts, but we are responsible for our thinking." It's normal for *wrong thoughts* to enter our minds from time to time. Our real concern should be *wrong thinking*.

It's not the random thought that should concern us. It's what we dwell on that matters. The Psalmist wrote, *"May the words of my mouth and <u>the meditation of my heart</u> be pleasing in your sight, O LORD, my Rock and my Redeemer"* (Psalms 19:14). Paradigms of defeat and unworthiness must be replaced with a new "can do" attitude. We should then meditate on thoughts that represent our new winning attitude.

Having clearly written goals helps mold our *mindset*. Our mind believes certain things and rejects others almost automatically based upon our mindset. Our renewed goal setting mindset should be "I can," "I will," "I have," and "I am." A good share of our beliefs and mindsets are formed in our childhood. We weren't afraid to believe and to pretend when we were children. But as we exit our youth and enter adulthood we begin to lose the freedom to dream and pretend. We take life too seriously, and forget that we were originally programmed to enjoy life. In Matthew 18:3, Jesus urged His followers to *"become as little children."*

When my (Eddie's) youngest son Bryan was five years old, we took him to a city park. We guided him as he climbed atop a ledge, about eight feet tall. I held up both arms and said with a smile, "Jump son. Daddy will catch you." Without hesitation, he flung himself into my arms. He truly *believed*.

The opposite of belief, *doubt* and *unbelief*, are the dream killers. If we begin to doubt the validity of our goals; question whether or not we can reach them; or begin to believe that we are unworthy, they won't come to pass. We must *master our minds*. We must decide to silence that little voice in our heads that says, "I can't do this. Who am I to think I deserve such success?" We dare not listen to it. It is not our true voice. It's a voice that's been programmed through the years to self-sabotage us and to keep us mired in a stagnated state of mediocrity. We must learn to ignore that voice and practice our own vocal programming habit of repeatedly saying and thinking positive things like, "I can do it. I will do it. I am doing it!" (Philippians 4:8)

> **Setbacks are part of the process—they are among the building blocks to our success!**

Face it: doubt is inevitable. It usually comes when challenges appear, or when we've suffered a setback. Remember, setbacks are part of the process—they are among the building blocks of our success! So, stand firm in your commitment. Kick doubt to the curb. Adopt a "no quit," "never-give-up" attitude.

This is not about motivational techniques. Motivational strategies are difficult to sustain. It is the *character* of a person who chooses to overcome that will sustain him through the tough times. It's our *victory mindset* that will help push us over the top. Overcoming setbacks builds our character and sets us up to conquer even greater things!

Let's move beyond the attitude that we are just warriors, and embrace the truth that we are "more than conquerors!" Conquerors take territory. As we gradually achieve greater measures of influence and success, we are conquering territory!

After conquering comes occupation. We become occupiers! We occupy the land, the area, and the dominion of our dreams. At that point we become, as Romans 8:37a says, *"more than conquerors."* We are to conquer, then occupy that for which we were created! The Bible puts it in these words. *"…Occupy till I come"* (Luke 19:13).

Faith

"Faith skips over the 'how.'"

Webster's Dictionary defines faith as *"belief not based on logical* (mental) *proof or material evidence."* Faith accepts a thing as true regardless of what our minds think. With faith there is a certainty that what we seek will become real. Faith skips over the "how." Faith is *"being sure of what you hope for and certain of that which you do not see."* (Hebrews 11:1)

As we've said, Jesus appreciated "child-likeness." Childlike faith eliminates impossibilities. We first accept our goals with childlike faith; then with *prayer* and *meditation* on the truth, we activate our faith to reach them.

Are we saying one should pray for faith? Absolutely! Romans 12:3-6 speak of one's "measure of faith" and the "proportion of faith" he's been given. In Mark, Chapter 9, we read the story of a man with a son who was vexed by an evil spirit. When Jesus told the desperate father that he should believe, he replied, *"Lord, I do believe; help me overcome my unbelief"* (Mark 9:24). He prayed (asked) for a greater measure of faith.

Meditate on the truth to increase your faith. Romans 10:17 tells us that faith comes from hearing the Word of God!

Think about this. Any time we ask for something that has not yet appeared, we are activating our faith. We are asking for that which is un-manifested to be manifested. This is one reason that we must be very careful what we ask for.

It's not just crazy people who talk to themselves. Everybody talks to himself or herself! We must also become aware of our self-talk. Having faith in what we want (our goals) gives us both substance and sustenance that what we hope for will indeed become reality.

For someone to say, "I have faith in you," means a lot. It is deeper than just hearing, "I believe in you." Faith equals trust. When we have faith in our goals we activate the supernatural and invite God into the matter.

> **God will have nothing to do with unbelief.**

Even the faith we place in ourselves and our dreams go beyond the natural. Faith reaches into the future and manifests it to us as real. If we lose faith in our goals and dreams we deactivate the supernatural. God will have nothing to do with unbelief. Hebrews 11:6 tells us that without it, we cannot please Him. Worse still, Romans 14:23 tells us that *"whatsoever is not of faith is sin!"*

Faith is seeing the end from the beginning. Because it skips the "how," faith allows us the grace not to have everything all figured out in advance. You may have heard some people refer to it as "blind faith." We aren't suggesting that faith is blind. It's not a "leap in the dark." It's a step in the Light.

> **Our dream is God's gift.**

Because we love God and He loves us and has put His desires in our hearts; our dream is His gift. Because our dream is a gift from Him, we receive it before we see it—out of faith in who He is! Consider this. If we were made aware, at the beginning of our journey, of all that we would face to reach our dream, we might not even take the first step.

In one sense, we live by faith whether we know it or not. When we drive, we have faith that the oncoming traffic will stay on their side of the road. When we flip the switch, we have faith that our lights will turn on. So when we have faith in our goals and dreams, we are essentially giving ourselves permission for "it to be so."

Along the journey we learn, as Paul taught us in 2 Corinthians 5:7, to live by faith and not by sight. You may say,

"This all sounds good, but if you only knew where I am, and the challenges I face, you'd understand why I can't... I can't..."

Well, let me (Kenn) encourage you. At 17 years of age I had nothing. "No-thing." I had no hope, no future, no money, and no possibilities. Mine was a dead-end life—reaching an early end. At a crucial life or death moment I decided that I would live by faith and trust that things would get better if I believed. I did, and my life changed. From that day 'til this, my dreams have come true and continue to come true. I love the new life I was given. It is not always easy, or without a struggle. At times it's quite challenging. But it is absolutely fulfilling!

> **Have faith in your highest aspirations.**

Faith is trust that springs from the heart. What you value is in your heart. As Christ taught, *"For where your treasure is, there your heart will be also"* (Matthew 6:21). I encourage you to live in a constant state of expectancy that your dreams and goals are indeed coming true. Have faith in your highest aspirations.

Hard work is also part of the equation. Work hard toward your goals because as James 2:16 says, *"faith by itself, if it does not have works, is dead."* If success in life and effective goal achievement were effortless, there would be little satisfaction with, or reason to celebrate the fulfillment.

The antithesis of faith is fear. While faith makes real what it is not yet seen in a positive sense, fear accepts what it does not yet see in a negative context. It's been said that f.e.a.r. is an acronym that stands for False Evidence Appearing Real. Not surprisingly perhaps, nearly every book in the Bible has a verse with the words *"fear not"* in it. Is God trying to tell us something? As faith is a *dream maker*, so fear is a *dream killer*.

Focus on faith and don't buy into fear. Stay in a state of unwavering faith and it will carry you through.

Know

*"Knowing is a quiet confidence that
what you want will come true"*

When we believe that our goal is valuable and worthwhile, and we have faith that it will come to pass, we begin to develop a peaceful inner knowing that it will be achieved. Webster's Dictionary defines *to know* as "to believe to be true with absolute certainty." When we know something to be true, we feel it deep down in our bellies—or as some would say it's a "gut" feeling.

Simply knowing our goal will become reality puts us more at ease. It gives us a sense of freedom, peace, and assurance that what we want will come to pass. Just knowing that our objective will manifest gives us unparalleled confidence to move forward to do our part to make it happen. Achievers live day-by-day knowing what they are striving for, and why. They know with a clear-cut confidence that it will become reality. Knowing gives them the fortitude to make it through the rough spots.

Great achievers tell us that they knew that what they were striving for would happen. It wasn't a matter of "if" it would happen, but "when" it would happen. It reminds me (Eddie) of a phrase that Jesus said, *"You shall know the truth and the truth shall make you free"* (John 8:32). Freedom however is not free. It requires strategy, planning, activation, hard work, and perseverance. Knowing that our dream will come to pass will make us unstoppable.

www.MaximumDreamAchievement.com

> **When we mentally link our goals with how reaching them will make us feel, we release a powerful effect.**

Let's review. Belief is mental. It works through logic—if this, then what? It considers cause and effect. Faith, which is found in the heart, resides in the realm of our feelings and emotions. We do much of what we do because of how it will make us feel. When we mentally link our goals with how reaching them will make us feel, we release a powerful effect.

Bind your logic (mental) with your emotions (heart). Say, "I *believe* with all my *heart* that __(Goal)__ will come true." As your dream becomes a "gut-level assurance" to you, it means you have "swallowed it whole" and it's becoming part of who you are—part of your identity.

Once again, please turn to the Action Exercise on page 119. Take a few minutes to complete it and then move on to Step 3 – Ink.

Chapter 4
Step Three – Ink

Write It / Speak It / Proclaim It

Write It

"...Write the vision and make it plain..."
(Habakkuk 2:2, ASV)

Writing down our goals is probably the single most important step we can take in effective goal setting. An unwritten goal is simply a "wish." It has no weight and carries no power. In Habakkuk 2:2 (The Message) we read, *"Write this. Write what you see. Write it out in big block letters so that it can be read on the run. This vision-message is a witness pointing to what's coming. It aches for the coming—it can hardly wait! And it doesn't lie. If it seems slow in coming, wait. It's on its way. It will come right on time."*

Written goals hurry toward their fulfillment. Many top achievers carry their written goals with them. They read them and re-read them throughout the day. I (Kenn) rewrite my goals every time I do my weekly and monthly To-Do lists. I suggest that you handwrite your goals too. It is remarkable what happens between the brain and the pen.

Writing is "to express and compose." Writing is a creative expression. When we handwrite a goal, we see it with our eyes as it appears on the paper. Handwriting our goals make them more real to us. This is why we encourage you to include writing throughout this 12-step goal setting process. Our written goals help hold us accountable to them.

Another reason that we write out our goals is so that we can look back at them in the future to see what was important to us at any particular season of life. I (Kenn) enjoy looking back at my goals journals from years past to see what I was striving for then.

One goal that I wrote years ago, that I found humorous, was "marry Michele," who was my girlfriend at the time. We've been happily married now for nearly two decades. Another was, "I want to be the Anthony Robbins of real estate." Anthony Robbins, as you may know, is a very popular bestselling author, success coach, and motivational speaker. Since writing down that goal, several years ago, I have sold several hundred millions of dollars in real estate as a direct result of my public speaking engagements. Honestly, writing out your goals will really become fun when you begin to see tangible results from doing so.

In my early twenties I was in a popular rock band called *The 5:15 Band*. At the time I thought we would shoot to superstardom. But ours was the typical story—our bass player quit, and our drummer got married. One of my handwritten goals at the time was to perform "live" in front of 35,000 people. That was a pretty lofty goal for an unknown band, right? Well, we were a great a capella vocal group that sang harmonious tunes (although I was the keyboard player and the only member of the band that did not sing).

We recorded our a capella version of *The Star Spangled Banner* and submitted it to major league baseball's Anaheim Angels. To our delight, they gave us a spot to perform the national anthem at Anaheim Stadium. When we got there it was surreal. Time stood still. Then to stand at home plate and perform our nation's theme song in front of 35,000 Angel fans was amazing. It was a goal almost supernaturally achieved.

What was even more amazing is that I sang the song with the band—even though I was not a singer. In fact, it was the first song I ever sang in public. Now that's the power of putting one's goals down on paper!

Speak It

It's important that we speak out our goal with confidence and conviction.

The next step is for us to begin to speak out our written goals. To "speak out" is to talk freely, fearlessly, unhesitatingly about them. The expressed spoken word carries great creative power. In Genesis 1:3 God **said,** *"Let there be light and there was."* It's important that we speak out our goals with confidence and conviction.

- When we speak our goals aloud we articulate them with our mouths. At the same time our ears hear them from the voice with which we are most familiar—our own.
- When we speak our goals aloud we create an atmosphere of increased trust and confidence.
- When we speak our goals, we can almost taste them. As is sometimes said of a thought, "It's on the tip of my tongue."

Our spoken words cause our goals to become more and more real to us.

Repetition is also important. We should affirm our goals every day—even several times a day. While driving or working we can affirm by repeating: "I am _(Goal)_ because _(Reason)_ so that _(Result)_ ." Extensive research has proven the power of spoken affirmations. Daily affirmations will change your life.

Affirmations

What are affirmations? Affirmations are short positive pronouncements that agree with our desired results. Once we hear ourselves repetitively affirm our positive desires and hoped for outcomes, we begin to believe them more fully. Our thoughts and daily actions will line up with our repeated affirmations.

Perhaps it's the musician in me, but I (Kenn) like affirmations that rhyme when possible, like, "I am happy and healthy in every way; I am getting better and better every day." Another one I use is, "I am easily and consistently closing two million in sales every month." Okay, so this one doesn't rhyme. But believe me; the months when I do reach that goal are like music to my pocket book!

Keep in mind that the result of speaking affirmations can also be used against us. Most of the thoughts we consider and the words we speak are (by default) based on our previous mental programming. Many of our negative conclusions, which shape our speech and thus our lives, were programmed in our minds during childhood, often unintentionally, by our parents and others. We should be careful what we say. What we say to ourselves (and to others) has a significant subconscious impact—especially negative words.

"No" is one of the first words we learn. That simple, two-letter word, overused in our childhood, often translates into paralysis in one's adult years. When our inner child says "wouldn't it be great to become _____?" The *"no"* in our subconscious can shut us down.

> **Our self-talk is so powerful it will greatly affect our destiny.**

Our self-talk is so powerful it will greatly affect our destiny. I (Kenn) witnessed this myself when my wife would relate a negative situation about another person or family. She had a habit of framing it with "I feel so bad that this happened…" or "I feel so bad they are in such trouble." She was trying to express compassion; but I realized that those four words, "I feel so bad…" were becoming a self-fulfilling prophesy. After saying to her friends "I feel so bad that your mom got sick," or "I feel so bad that you didn't get the job," she literally started feeling bad, and at times quite seriously.

Similarly, our positive self-talk and affirmations have a powerful positive impact on our future. Our subconscious minds automatically align with our spoken commands. This isn't psychobabble—it's real. The good news is that we can re-program negative self-talk with positive, consistent, repetitive affirmations; and by speaking our written goals and aspirations. Take a moment and make a commitment to make positive, life-giving affirmations throughout your day. Make it your lifestyle. It will change your life—really!

Reinforcement

As we've said, it's important that we speak out our written goals on a daily or at least a weekly basis. Simply take out your goals journal and read them aloud with confidence. Avoid words like "try" or "might." Our minds subconsciously know that "trying is lying." We must constantly reinforce the goals we've set. Whether or not they seem to be coming to pass as expected is not our concern.

Our objective is to speak our desired positive results with conviction. Conviction means "convinced." The more we speak our goals the more convinced of them we become. Or perhaps the more we *hear* our goals spoken, the more convinced we become. Remember, according to Romans 10:17, *"faith comes by hearing."* Are you convinced that your goals are worthy of pursuit? Then speak them regularly and with conviction.

Where do we speak our goals and affirmations? Some of us do so in front of a mirror. Some record them multiple times and regularly listen to the recording. Others of us speak them when we're driving. It is best to speak them when no one is around. That way we can speak loudly and convincingly, proving to ourselves that our dreams are coming to pass.

> **Speaking our goals and affirmations quietly, almost imperceptibly, is also effective.**

Sometimes I (Kenn) review my goals in crowded restaurants. Of course that's not the most appropriate place to speak loudly to myself. But here's a little-known secret. For us to speak our goals and affirmations quietly, almost imperceptibly, can also be effective.

It's like when your kids are out of control and you've not succeeded in convincing them of what you want them to do with your louder more commanding voice. It can often be effective if you kneel down in front of them, look them straight in the eyes, and with a quiet but firm voice explain what you want. At that point my kids usually get the point. So use those times when you can't speak out loudly to speak your goals and affirmations quietly, yet firmly, to yourself like a serious parent implementing discipline.

Proclaim It

"...For out of the heart, the mouth speaks" (Matthew 12:34)
– Jesus.

Once we've written our goals and repeatedly spoken them aloud, we should *proclaim them*. The word "proclaim" is from the Latin word, *proclamare*. "Pro" is a prefix that means *before*. "Clamare" is Latin for *to cry out*. To proclaim means to "claim in advance." To claim something is to call it your own — to take possession of something you already own.

It's similar to our claiming an inheritance that is rightfully ours. All we must do is step up and claim it. When we proclaim that our goal is to have "X" amount of income or achieve "X" pounds of body weight gained or lost, we are seeing and claiming it in advance, declaring or making it known formally and officially. To declare our goals is to "set them in stone," and to proclaim them allows all to hear what is to be.

Consider how powerful and effective America's *Declaration of Independence* and *The Emancipation Proclamation* were when they were officially presented. Those who signed the *Declaration of Independence*, risked everything for what they believed. Although many of them were wealthy businessmen and landowners, by signing *The Declaration* they were formally announcing to the King of England, "Our goal of independence is a do or die matter." They knew that if they lost the fight they would lose everything and quite possibly lose their lives.

> **Proclaim your goals aloud and with conviction to the important goal-oriented people in your life.**

When President Abraham Lincoln signed and read aloud *The Emancipation Proclamation*, he put his political career and the future of our nation on the line for the goal of freedom for all men. We should have the same conviction regarding our important life altering goals and proclaim them aloud, even publicly.

When we made it a goal to write this book, we proclaimed it to our wives, families, friends, and co-workers. We proclaimed it at the seminars we were teaching. We "shouted it out aloud." Proclaiming it also kept us accountable. We had many people (even those we didn't know) ask, "How's the book coming?" Proclaim your goals aloud and with conviction to the important goal-oriented people in your life.

Please take time to do the Action Exercise on page 120. It will make your day!

Chapter 5
Step Four – Motives

List Benefits / List Consequences / Motivations

List Benefits

"For the joy set before Him (Jesus)..."
(Hebrews 12:2)

Next it's important that we recognize *the benefits* we expect to enjoy as a result of achieving our goals. Benefits are the rewards we receive for our efforts. How will achieving our goals make us feel? What new opportunities will our having achieved our goals open up for us? This verse from Hebrews (above) reveals to us a benefit that Jesus anticipated, which caused Him to willingly die on the cross for us. Here is the complete sentence: *"...For the joy set before him he endured the cross, scorning its shame, and sat down at the right hand of the throne of God."*

Every decision we make is made on the basis of emotion. We do what we feel like doing then justify it later in our minds. It's also true that we do what we do for the benefits we expect to receive. Begin now to attach your emotions to the future benefits you anticipate.

Close your eyes and imagine yourself achieving or receiving the benefits you expect. Smile, or for that matter, laugh out loud. The more beneficial you perceive achieving your goals to be, the more likely you will desire and diligently work to accomplish them. Think of the rewards big and small that you expect once your goals are achieved.

> **To list our anticipated benefits is to describe our inheritance.**

The word *benefits* relates to the word "beneficiary." A beneficiary is one who receives an inheritance. When we list the benefits to come, we are describing our inheritance. We would expect that an inheritance would make our lives easier, ease our financial burdens, and allow us a greater measure of freedom. So we should take our inheritance seriously.

Go ahead. List all the good things that will result as you accomplish your goals. Get creative. Let's have fun with your benefits lists. If it benefits you it will most likely benefit others as well. List others who will benefit as you reach your goals. "I have my children's college education paid for by (date)." List the benefits for you, for your family, and others.

Remember, the benefits we expect to receive once our goals are met will motivate us toward their completion. When we realize how many others will benefit from our efforts we'll have a higher sense of purpose, one beyond personal ambition alone. When things get tough and we lose our focus along the way, which at times happens to us all, we can review our benefits lists and be re-motivated by what awaits us upon reaching our goals.

Our periodic reviews of the benefits list in our goals journal will help us through the tough times. It's then that we can say to ourselves, "Okay, now I remember why I am doing this." Fun stuff!

If earning a million dollars in one year is your goal, write down what accomplishing that will mean to you, to your family, your church, or other charities that you support. If owning a beautiful beachfront condo in Hawaii is your goal, what benefits would that provide? Make your list:

1. A place to recharge
2. A place to bond with my family on vacation
3. A property that I can leave to my children or grandchildren when I pass
4. A good investment for future appreciation and income, and on and on...

List Consequences

People do what they do for two basic motivators: to gain pleasure (benefits); or to avoid pain (consequences). So, our next step is for us to consider the consequences of what might happen if we don't achieve our goals. What would it cost us?

How about to avoid regret? Imagine yourself turning eighty-years-old, looking back and saying, "If I only I had done this or that, how different my life would be today." Now bring that thought into the present and say, "If I don't take this action now, I will end up like this _____?_____..."

For example, if your goal is to stop smoking, list the likely consequences of not doing so.

www.MaximumDreamAchievement.com

> **The pain of loss is a greater motivator than the pleasure of gain.**

My (Kenn's) mother smoked two packs of cigarettes a day. As a result, she died in her early forties. One primary consequence of her untimely death is that we don't get to share the wonderful moments of our lives with her today. We don't want to spend too much time on the negative, but the future consequences of unmet goals, and unrealized dreams could very well be the catalyst we need to motivate us. The pain of loss is actually a greater motivator than the pleasure of gain. Attaching painful results to our failing to reach our goals will spur us on.

From time to time we make seemingly insignificant decisions that aren't aligned with our preferred future and we end up off course. Little things do matter!

Our written goals and plans help us make better choices. We each have the power to choose—free will. If we had known ahead of time the results of many of our past choices, we might never have chosen them. Let's become "consequence-aware."

Every choice we make has both short- and long-term results. I (Kenn) can't tell you how many versions of *A Christmas Carol* I have read or watched, but the moral of that classic tale is one we should each take to heart.

In the story, the miserly character Scrooge was transformed once he saw the future results of his past choices. We may well be transformed when we acknowledge the losses that would result of our goals not achieved.

www.MaximumDreamAchievement.com

Motivations

Benefits and consequences motivate us to get moving, to put into motion. To sustain our motivation we should constantly remind ourselves of the benefits and consequences.

We suggest that you look for an accountability partner or achievement coach who will provide you with continual encouragement and help hold you accountable to your goals. Motivational seminars are wonderful but their effectiveness fades fairly quickly. The very best athletes, at the highest levels of their sport, have performance and personal coaches. Find or hire someone you trust to help you stay motivated and moving forward.

Post your goals and benefits list on your mirror. Put them on your screen saver. I (Kenn) shared this strategy one night at the dinner table with my family, and my son Justin took my advice. He was on the freshman basketball team at the time, and had scored only four points during his previous game.

Justin then made it his written goal to make twenty points. In a few days, they were going to play the same team that they had played the previous week. Justin listed the benefits of his scoring twenty points, and the consequences of failing to do so. Sure enough, he achieved his twenty-point goal. Needless to say, Justin is a believer in the motivational power of goal setting and listing benefits.

Get Uncomfortable

> **We *must* become uncomfortable with being too comfortable.**

Each of us tends to revert to complacency—to that which is comfortable. If we are to succeed in life and in business, we *must* become uncomfortable with being too comfortable.

For us to expand and stretch ourselves requires effort and sometimes produces pain. Ask anyone who hires a trainer to help him or her become physically fit. A trainer will push his clients beyond what is comfortable. He does that because the majority of positive results come from the last few repetitions of each exercise.

Our *motives* are our underlying reasons for doing what we do. They are tied directly to what we expect our reward to be. Some refer to it as our "big why." Routinely reviewing our desired results and motivations will help push us down the track like a living example of the children's story, *The Little Train That Could*.

We should repeat to ourselves: "I *know* I can, I *know* I can." (Not "I *think* I can.") True motivation is saying, "I *know* I can." Face it. Goal achievement is a battle. But it is a good fight that we must engage in every day. We must fight for our dream every day. The Apostle Paul encourages us to *"fight the good fight of faith"* (1 Timothy 6:12) Fighting is rarely comfortable, but it is required.

As we continue to fight we'll eventually conqueror. As stated earlier, we're not merely survivors in this thing called *life*. Not at all. According to the Apostle Paul, we are *"more than conquerors"* (Romans 8:37).

In a parable that Jesus taught in Luke 19, He said in verse thirteen, *"…occupy 'till I come."* To succeed we must not only conquer, we must *occupy!* Once we have taken the territory of our destiny we then earn the privilege to occupy it and to live our dream. Your preferred future is worth fighting for. Get comfortable with being uncomfortable. The fight is on!

Take a few moments and complete the Action Exercise on page 121. You will be glad you did.

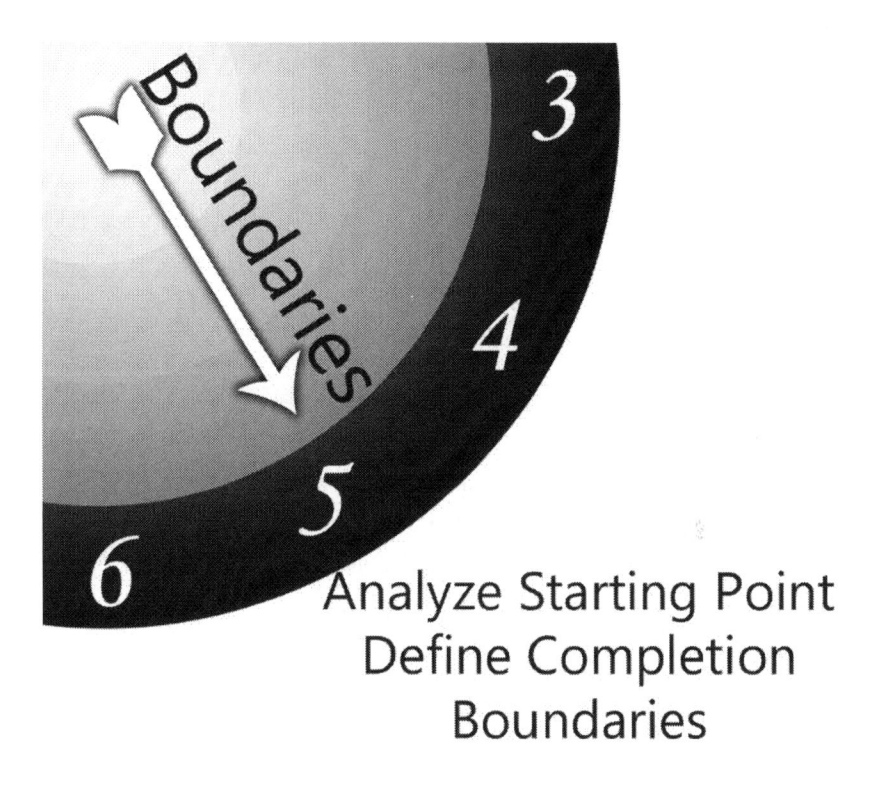

Analyze Starting Point
Define Completion
Boundaries

Chapter 6
Step Five – Boundaries

Analyze Starting Point / Define Completion / Boundaries

"The boundary lines have fallen for me in the pleasant places; surely I have a delightful inheritance"
(Psalm 16:6)

The fifth step in our goal setting process is for us to analyze our starting point. To *analyze* means, "to break something down into its elemental parts." Before going on a mountain climbing expedition you would surely lay out all of your gear to see what you have and what is missing. When we set out on a mission or start a project we should break down and categorize the resources that we have to begin with.

www.MaximumDreamAchievement.com

I (Kenn) remember when I was a child how my father would take us hunting or fishing. Before we left we would lay all of the gear we would need on the garage floor. Then we would test each piece. We usually had most of what we needed, but inevitably a few crucial items would be missing. It might have ruined our trip had we not inspected everything ahead of time.

Once we discovered what was missing we would go buy it, or we'd pick it up along the way rather than go into the field without it.

Thousands of years ago, Jesus said, *"Suppose one of you wants to build a tower. Will he not first sit down and estimate the cost to see if he has enough money to complete it"* (Luke 14:28)?

My (Eddie) father once asked me, "Son, if you are about to take a trip to Chicago and I hand you a map, what's the first thing you look for?"

Easy, I thought. I said, "Dad, the first thing I'd look for is Chicago."

> **We must first establish our starting point.**

He replied, "No, son. The first thing you should look for is your present location. Once you clearly see where you are, only *then* should you look for your proposed destination—Chicago."

For example, if your goal is to become financially free, you must first analyze your current financial status. You might start with a simple asset and liability statement to show your net worth. Then analyze your monthly profit and loss statements to see your income and expenses. So determine first to establish your starting point.

You may need to consult an advisor who can tell you what is missing in your analysis. For many years I (Kenn) was the president of a mortgage company. When I took a loan application from a borrower there would be a checklist of all the items that were needed to complete the loan package. However, inevitably there would be missing items. I would give my clients a list of the missing documents so they could go home and retrieve them. We couldn't complete the funding of the loan without all the documents being in place.

The good news is that you may realize that you already have more in place than you think. When I made it my goal to earn my real estate broker's license the state required me to have a certain number of college hours in core subjects as well as non-core subjects. When I broke down and analyzed what classes the state required I found that several courses I had taken in college satisfied the state's requirements. This saved me countless hours of additional classes that I would have had to otherwise complete.

Don't be discouraged however if you don't have the necessary resources at hand. Most of us start our journeys with limited resources and knowledge. That's okay because we can quickly discover what we need, what to do, and where to go to obtain what's required.

Let's be honest with ourselves as we begin, and not allow humble beginnings to hold us back. Zechariah 4:10 encourages us not to "despise" small beginnings.

Define Completion

> **Some people set goals that are so ambiguous; they are never quite sure when they've reached them.**

It is important that we describe what our goals will look like once they are achieved. Some people set such ambiguous goals that they are never quite sure when they've reached them. "I want to be rich" is not a specific goal. A clearly defined goal would be, "I have $1 million cash in the bank by age 55."

A soccer player's fancy footwork as he runs towards the goal with the ball doesn't matter. Ultimately, the thing that matters is to get the ball into the net.

There is great satisfaction in knowing exactly what you want to achieve, then going for it. Day-by-day, week-by-week, as you move towards your target, you'll know precisely when you have hit the mark.

Mission Statement

Our minds, our wills, and our emotions work much better when we write out our clear-cut goals and well-defined preferred outcomes. That is our *mission statement*. It helps us define *completion*.

Your mission statement could be: "I happily help 50 disadvantaged inner-city children become successful entrepreneurs through educational and inspirational programs." Or perhaps it could be: "I help to provide 20 college scholarships each year through government sponsored programs and philanthropic organizations." How will you know your goal is achieved? Easy. You'll know it is achieved when the 20th kid enrolls in college with his or her scholarship.

Our mission statements need to be descriptive, clear, and concise. Here's an example:

> *The mission of the Big Brothers and Big Sisters of America is to make a positive difference in the lives of children and youth, primarily through a professionally supported, one-to-one relation-ship with a caring adult, and to assist them in achieving their highest potential as they grow to become confident, competent, and caring individuals by*

providing committed volunteers, national leadership, and standards of excellence.

My (Kenn's) mission statement is:

Living, loving, and growing in the purposes God has for me and helping others to do the same.

My (Eddie and his wife, Alice's) ministry mission statement is:

Discipling nations by equipping Christian leaders.

Go ahead. Write a short, powerful, engaging mission statement for each of your important goals.

Vision Statement

Our *vision statement* is a paragraph or two that describes, in detail, the future reality of our completed goal. It defines the emotions and feelings of satisfaction that we will experience once we've achieved our goal.

> **"Begin with the end in mind."**

Carefully consider your vision statement "a snapshot" of that future day. Imagine it. Envision it.

Don't allow this step to throw you. Proverbs 23:7 teaches that as we think, we are, and we become. Our meditation is an important spiritual component of our success.

Go ahead. Find a quiet spot, close your eyes and peer mentally into the near or even the distant future as if to watch "a private mental movie" of the day when you've reached your goal. What do you *see*? Who's with you? What circumstances surround you on that day—in that moment?

What changes are you experiencing as you see your goal reached? Write out what you envision. Describe who is with you on that day. This now is your vision statement. As noted author, the late Stephen Covey stated, "Begin with the end in mind."

Boundaries

Along with our knowing where we are (our starting point), and where we are going (our completed goal), it's important that we define our boundaries.

The boundary lines define whether or not we are "in the game." As life would have it, many times we think we are on track toward reaching a goal, only to discover that we've drifted away. We can easily get distracted and "foul out." We must be discerning enough to know clearly when we are in the game, and when we are not.

During the process of achieving a goal it's helpful, as we've said, to have a coach or accountability partner help us stay "in bounds." In sports, the field of play is well defined. For example, at times we may think we are really making progress only to find out that we are actually missing the mark, which is like golfing in the wrong fairway. It's like working on a savings plan and then overspending. It does no good to save diligently for a year only to blow double the amount we've saved on a new ski boat, and still think we're "getting ahead."

We know. We've both been in that boat before. Honestly, we too struggle with staying inbounds. We don't always like boundaries but we know they are there for a reason. They are to alert us when we're drifting and to keep us on the playing field. Those who refuse to live within the boundaries are destined to live lives of mediocrity or even disaster.

As our influence expands, through achieving more and more, we will find "our playing fields" enlarging. Our competition gets stiffer as we step into higher levels of achievement. When our boundaries expand and we exert ourselves to the extreme, we break through the ranks and head into open, sometimes unknown territory. Yes, we will experience setbacks along the way. But remember, setbacks are only temporary. When you get knocked down, get up, brush yourself off and get moving again. The goal line is just a few steps away. Staying inbounds is a result of continually reviewing and analyzing our results along the way.

> **Life is meant to be a goal-achieving journey.**

What does a mountaineer see when he reaches the summit? Yep, he discovers that there are yet more mountains to climb. So guess what happens once you reach your goal? That's right! There will be another exciting goal waiting to be achieved. *Life is meant to be a goal-achieving journey.* Make the most of it and enjoy the ride. Sure, there will be struggles along the way; but there is victory in the end. Never ever give up!

Please go to page 123 and do the Action Exercise.

www.MaximumDreamAchievement.com

Set a Deadline
Set a Starting Date
The Stopwatch

Chapter 7
Step Six - Time

Set a Deadline / Set a Starting Date / The Stopwatch

*"For everything there is a season,
a time for every activity under Heaven"*
(Ecclesiastes 3:1)

Set a Deadline

If we are to succeed we must set a written, specific deadline for the completion of each goal. Our subconscious minds work automatically to meet deadlines. The most points in professional football are scored in the final two minutes of each half. Why is that? It is because the teams are more focused and energized when faced with specific impending deadlines. Without deadlines we can easily succumb to any of a number of anti-goal achieving activities such as procrastination and distraction. It is easy for us to put off important things and trade our time for more menial and even unnecessary activities.

> **It is easy for us to be busy, yet ineffective.**

Busyness is a rampant scourge in today's society. It is easy for us to be busy and accomplish little or nothing. It's necessary that we move from being busy to being effective. We should constantly ask ourselves, "Is this what I should be doing right now? Is it the most effective use of my time?"

Deadlines are productivity motivators. Did you ever cram late night for a final exam? How much do you get done the few days prior to leaving on a two-week vacation? Can you imagine how effective our lives would be if we worked like we were about to leave on a long vacation? When we prepare for such a trip we list the things we'll need; we make sure that our pets are cared for; we check items off our lists as we get them done. We focus all the more as the deadline approaches.

We know the specific day and time our plane is to depart—a deadline. Deadlines are good. The world operates according to deadlines. Does April 15th ring a bell? Of course it does. Deadlines rule!

So what happens if we don't meet the deadline? We simply set another deadline. However, to know that we can extend a deadline is not an invitation for us to procrastinate. Even when writing this book we've both played the "busyness card." We established deadlines. We hit some and missed others. When we missed a writing deadline we'd set another deadline and strive to meet it. Why? We did so because we knew this book would change lives for the better—hopefully yours as well. It's not something that we took lightly. We felt commissioned to write this book. A publisher told me (Kenn) that a half-written book is no book at all. That was a wake up call for me to get back to writing to meet my deadline.

Set a Starting Date

We need to have a start date as well as a deadline. It's important that we commit to begin our "goal journey" on a certain date—a commencement date. It's easy for us to set goals, and even create plans to achieve them, yet never get started.

Write down your starting date and resolve to take your first action step on that date. It could be as simple as picking up the phone and making a call, or stepping outside to take your first long healthy walk.

We suggest that you not make New Year's Day your starting date. Why? The reason is that there are more resolutions broken on January 2nd than on any other day of the year. How about starting your dream-achieving goal now? Why now? There is power in *now*. To say, "I am starting today" is a very motivating and engaging.

Whatever you decide; set your *start date*. Then on that day, review your goals journal. Engage all of your "whys." Remind yourself of what you are going to do and why you will be doing it. Then pull the trigger, fire the starting gun, and start to run down the track.

The Stopwatch

Do you remember how the television show *60 Minutes* begins? It begins with a visual of a stopwatch and the sound—tick, tick, tick. When you see and hear that watch you know the

www.MaximumDreamAchievement.com

show has begun and a sixty-minute presentation is ticking away. The stopwatch reminds us before and after each commercial break that we are watching *60 Minutes.*

Once we set a deadline for our goal and determine our starting date, it becomes like that stopwatch. Go! Tick, tick, tick… The stopwatch has no feelings. It is neither biased nor lenient. It simply keeps track of the race we are running. The stopwatch doesn't lie. It compares our performances to our past similar performances or to others who have run the same or a similar race.

Once we begin we should take action steps every day toward our goal, and keep moving toward our preferred future. We must not stop fighting for the cause. After all, our future or our lives may depend on it. Our goals will be achieved only if we are willing to push past the limits of our current capacity.

I (Kenn) am reminded of those cheesy southwestern desert postcards I used to see on road trips. It would be a staged photograph of a pioneer's skeleton just inches away from reaching his water canteen. Your victory may be only inches or minutes away from you today. It's common for us to want to give up at the last minute—don't you do it! Press in, press on—your victory may just be "one tick away."

The Apostle Paul reminds us, *"Do you not know that in a race all the runners run, but only one gets the prize? Run in such a way as to get the prize."* (1 Corinthians 9:24).

Do not hesitate…go to page 124 and do the Action Exercise.

List Obstacles
Identify Opportunities
Survey Territory

Chapter 8
Step Seven - Survey

List Obstacles / Identify Opportunities / Survey Territory

List Obstacles

"Look the land over, see what it is like"
(Numbers 13:17-20)

Every journey comes complete with its own share of obstacles. The bigger the goal, the greater the obstacles we'll encounter. However, let's not allow life's obstacles to prevent us from pursuing and ultimately reaching our dreams. Resistance is a healthy and necessary part of any endeavor.

Suppose you met me (Eddie) on the street one day and I had my right arm in a sling. You might ask, "Eddie, why are you wearing the sling? Did you injure your arm?"

To which I might reply, "No, not at all. You see, I'm planning to enter the Senior Olympics as a javelin thrower. Between now and then, I'm saving up all the energy I can muster so that I can win."

Silly, isn't it? We know that the only way to strengthen muscles is to stress them. Resistance, not rest, causes growth.

When obstacles are defined they become quantifiable, measureable, and less intimidating. When we identify the obstacles they become smaller in our minds. To identify the known obstacles will enable us to begin the "overcoming process."

> **Listing known obstacles removes the fear**

Fear is a great de-motivator. Fear of what's *known* can certainly be debilitating; but fear of the *unknown* is a killer. It leads to stress, and ultimately to paralysis. Listing our known obstacles helps remove the fear factor. Once we see what we need to overcome, our subconscious minds automatically begin seeking solutions.

As mentioned earlier, throughout the Bible God encourages His people to "fear not." He knows that fear will lead us astray. Medically fear, and the stress caused by fear, can lead to an early death.

The question is not *"if* I will overcome the obstacles," but *"how will I* overcome the obstacles." The great explorers Lewis and Clark had to trek across mountain ranges, raging rivers, marshes, and deserts. Theirs was never a question of *if* they would succeed. Instead it was *how* they would do so. Their commitment was to "do or die." When we attach that kind of passion and level of commitment to overcoming our obstacles, there's no limit to where we can go and what we can do.

The Point of No Return

When Columbus and other Atlantic explorers sailed toward the Americas from Europe there was a point in the journey where the captain had to make a choice of whether to continue on to the New World or turn back. That was the point where they had just enough food and supplies to make it back to the European mainland, if they were to turn back. It was called "the point of no return." Talk about courage! Remember, even if they continued there was no guarantee that they would reach land.

Explorers had to overcome fear of the unknown as well as other obstacles they would eventually encounter. One of the primary obstacles that lay ahead for them was called "the doldrums." The doldrums occur in parts of the Atlantic at certain times of the year when the winds cease to blow. There wasn't enough wind to fill their sails and push them on toward their goals.

> Don't worry – the winds will blow again.

From time to time we too will face the doldrums along our journey of goal-achievement. Remember, they are temporary. When we experience the doldrums, we should refrain from making any major decisions. Those are times we should kick back, think of the future, go swimming and pray for the winds of change to blow sooner rather than later to get us back in motion. They eventually do.

To wait for a breakthrough is sometimes part of the process. After His resurrection Jesus told His disciples not to leave Jerusalem, but to wait for the special gift of His Holy

Spirit. They waited patiently for 50 days to receive the Holy Spirit. Because they did, their lives were never the same, and they became world changers!

Obstacles are opportunities for growth and character development. When mountains block our way or raging rivers slow our progress, it's time for us to come up with solutions. Those challenges should shift us into thinking creatively. When your problems seem insurmountable, remember Lewis and Clark. They faced it all and overcame. So our persistence and creativity will help us navigate over, through and around the obstacles that we will encounter. Overcoming makes us stronger, more experienced, and builds our confidence.

The Apostle Paul was certainly familiar with obstacles and overcoming them, and in 2 Corinthians 11, verses 23 to 27 (The Message) he recalls a few of them. Paul says...

> *I've worked much harder, been jailed more often, beaten up more times than I can count, and at death's door time after time. I've been flogged five times with the Jews' thirty-nine lashes, beaten by Roman rods three times, pummeled with rocks once. I've been shipwrecked three times, and immersed in the open sea for a night and a day. In hard traveling year in and year out, I've had to ford rivers, fend off robbers, struggle with friends, struggle with foes. I've been at risk in the city, at risk in the country, endangered by desert sun and sea storm, and betrayed by those I thought were my brothers. I've known drudgery and hard labor, many a long and lonely night without sleep, many a missed meal, blasted by the cold, naked to the weather.*

In spite of it all, Paul declares in Philippians 4:11-13 (The Message), *"I've learned by now to be quite content whatever my circumstances. I'm just as happy with little as with much, with much as with little. I've found the recipe for being happy whether full or hungry, hands full or hands empty. Whatever I have, wherever I am, I can make it through anything in the One who makes me who I am."*

Identify Opportunities

We are surrounded with opportunities. When we become goal-oriented we become both opportunity seekers and opportunity-magnets. We've all had the experience of buying a car of a particular brand or color; only to begin to see (for the first time) similar cars as ours. Of course they were there all along. It was only after buying our car that we began to see them.

When I (Kenn) start my day, I often ask myself, "What opportunities will I find today that will improve my life or the lives of others?" We suggest that you make a list of the current opportunities of which you are aware that will help you meet your goal.

The root meaning of the word *opportunity* is "to port." A port is a hub of trade and commerce. Ships come in from distant lands and deliver their cargo at the port. Rail lines and transportation companies bring raw and manufactured goods to the port so they can be loaded on ships for passage to other parts of the world. The ships and crews get re-supplied with fuel and provisions at the port. Ports are filled with new opportunities and possibilities.

What goods and services can you trade? What can you bring to port? What will you offer in trade for the things you need? I (Eddie) served in the U.S. Navy. I know what it's like to live at sea for weeks at a time. When we sailed the high seas all we saw was the wide-open ocean—water! However all kinds of possibilities presented themselves when we pulled into port.

"Ports" in our business lives include networking meetings, trade shows, industry business conferences, and office meetings. Go ahead and list all of the great ideas or products that you feel might complement your effort to reach goals. You may find a problem solving solution in a book, a presentation, or in a seminar. I (Kenn) met one of my best friends and business partners while visiting a booth at a Home and Garden show.

Each of us should continually look for opportunities with an open mind, especially when we're short on ideas. Then we should sort them and select only the best opportunities for our objectives. When we become goal-oriented entrepreneurs, more and more opportunities will present themselves. Warning! Many of those opportunities will look good; but as author Jim Collins states, "Good is the enemy of great."

We'll soon have more opportunities than we have time, energy, or money to pursue. That's why we attempt to choose only the *right* opportunities. Chasing "okay" or "kind of cool" ideas will distract us from greatness.

| Be brilliant at the basics. |

One of the most often overlooked opportunities we each have is to become really proficient at our current responsibilities. We call this principle: *Being brilliant at the basics*.

Take me (Kenn) for example. I'm a real estate broker. Lead generation, which is to identify and call on prospects, is a core duty of mine. My teams' goal is to generate leads a minimum of three hours per working day. Although that sounds like a lot, it's only 15 hours out of a 40 or 50-hour workweek. I admit that we sometimes struggle to meet that goal, but I know that it's crucial to our success. So, I make it a daily priority.

Interestingly, when we start heading toward an objective our attention is immediately drawn toward things we might normally have missed. I remember when it was time to expand my real estate offices. Suddenly I began to see office space signs everywhere. They had been there all along, but I hadn't seen them until I started focusing on my goal. Office spots seemed to pop out everywhere. The same will hold true when you head towards your goal. What you focus on will expand. The signs of opportunity will begin to appear. Just make sure you choose the best ones. Make a list of the obstacles and opportunities that are currently associated with your upcoming journey.

Survey Territory

Our next step is to survey the territory into which we are about to move. To *survey* is to "look something over." The territory is the land, the region, and spheres of influence in an area.

You have listed the obstacles and the opportunities. Now take a 10,000-foot view of the territory.
- Who occupies the land now?
- Where are the steepest climbs?
- Is the money that's necessary for you to proceed a challenge for you?
- Where on this map will you find sources of funds?

I (Kenn) have helped thousands of home buyers become home owners. Part of my responsibility is to sit down with my clients to discuss the "territory." We talk not only

www.MaximumDreamAchievement.com

about where they want to live, but also how they are going to get there. Sometimes coming up with a down payment can be a challenge.

In one case, my clients were about $1,000 short of being able to close on a home purchase. We surveyed their assets and found out that they had inherited a horse (remember, we're in Texas). The horse was worth $1,200. We were able to sell the horse and meet the down payment requirements. They now own a home with money they found by surveying their "territory."

I (Eddie) have a friend who has an orphanage in Louisiana. One day he was very concerned. There wasn't enough money for groceries. While praying about how he would feed his thirty children, he noticed a pecan fall to the ground. Suddenly, he realized that his lot was filled with ripe pecans.

When the children came home from school that day, they harvested the pecans, which they sold for $200! The pecans had been there all along. He just needed to "survey the land."

> **Properly executed, coaching works.**

If our goal is to achieve financial independence through investing, we need to mentally survey "the land."

- What is the current economic climate?
- Where are the best locations to invest?
- What financial challenges will need to be overcome?

Keep in mind that you may need to engage the services of a coach, a guide, or an advisor to help quicken your journey. A good coach already knows the terrain and can help you. Business coaching is big business, and for good reason. Properly executed, coaching works.

It is also important to determine who currently occupies "the territory." For instance, if your goal is to be elected as mayor or to run for congress you'll want to survey the current regime and any other potential candidates.

- What are their spheres of influence in that territory?
- Who has been successful?
- Who is corrupt?
- Who influences the influencers?

In Numbers 13:17-20 the Lord commanded Moses to instruct the people to:

> "Look the land over, <u>see what it is like</u>. Assess the people: are they strong or weak? Are there few or many? Observe the land: is it pleasant or harsh? Describe the towns where they live: are they open camps or fortified walls? And the soil: is it fertile or barren? Are there forests?"

When you survey ahead of time you'll have a bird's eye view of the territory you are about to conquer.

Take a minute and go to page 125 and do the Action Exercise.

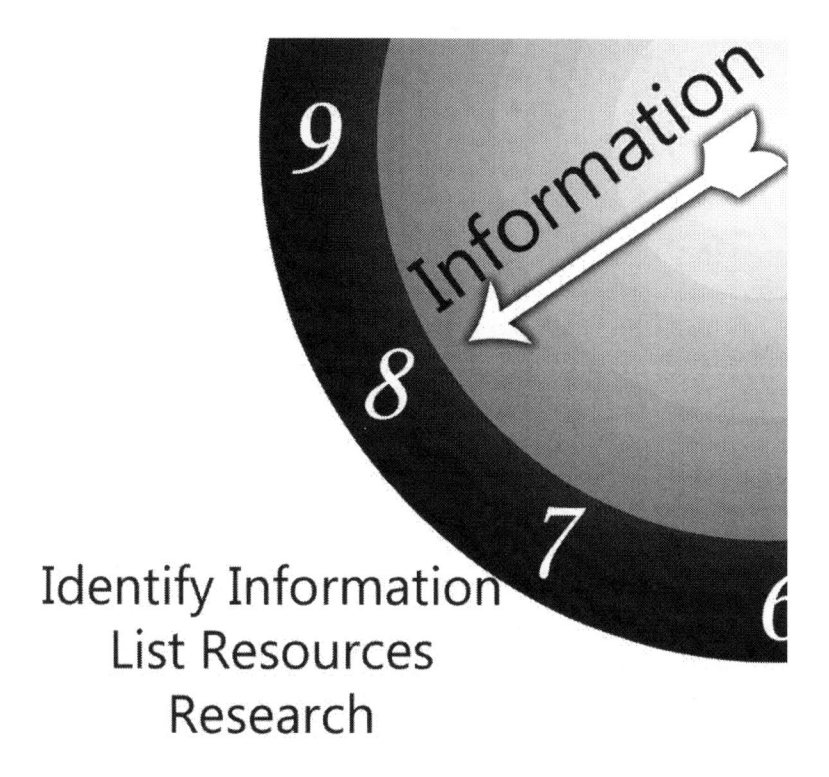

Identify Information
List Resources
Research

Chapter 9
Step Eight - Information

Identify Information / List Resources / Research

"Wisdom is supreme; therefore get wisdom"
(Proverbs 4:7)

Identify Information

To *research* is to "diligently investigate a matter." In our youth, we had to do research at a library. However, in today's Internet age, information and instructions on how to do virtually anything are as close as a click of a mouse, or a tap on one's smart phone. Billions of informative web pages and videos are at our fingertips on our smart phones.

Recently, I (Kenn) was about to grill chicken on our barbeque. In the past, I've tended to overcook chicken when grilling. In fact, at times our kids have referred to my results as "chicken jerky."

This time, tired of my past grilling failures, I searched *YouTube* on my smart phone for the phrase: "how to grill chicken." I watched a seven-minute instructional video, then I followed the instructions, and *voila!* We enjoyed a great chicken dinner.

When I decided that I would become a millionaire, I studied books like *Think and Grow Rich, The Millionaire Next Door,* and *The Secrets of the Millionaire Mind.* I identified books that had helped others become millionaires and followed their advice. Within a few years, I was in "the millionaire's club."

List Resources

The information is out there and it's easier than ever to access. In your goals journal, list the information resources that will best assist, inspire, and challenge you to reach your goal. Internet websites, books, audio series, seminars, trade shows, and networking are all great places for you to gather knowledge.

If your goal is to obtain your real estate license, you will need to gather the appropriate books and courses that will help you pass your test. A list of required courses will be found on your state's real estate agency website. If your goal is to obtain a bachelor's degree, make a list of the courses and requirements needed to achieve that goal.

Success leaves trails. We can research success stories and discover what others have done to achieve goals like ours. Better yet, we can find successful people and invite them to lunch and pick their brains as to how they became successful.

Ask what information and resources he or she found most helpful. What books did they read? What classes did they attend? Keep a file of your findings.

Webster's Dictionary defines *information* as "knowledge derived from study, experience, or instruction." We need not "re-write the book." Most likely others have already done what we want to do (or at least something similar). Find them. Take their course, read their books, attend their seminars, or as we've said, invite them to lunch.

The Apostle Paul, in his letter to the Christians in Philippi wrote: *"Whatever you have learned or received or heard from me, or seen in me—put it into practice. And the God of peace will be with you"* (Philippians 4:9). He offered himself to them as a living example—a pattern for life.

Although the Apostle Paul died centuries ago, his example and counsel continues to benefit us today. Some of the information in this book is derived from ancient writings, the Holy Bible, the dictionary, sermons we've heard, seminars we've attended, audio and video programs we've purchased, and other sources.

Even more powerful than knowledge is wisdom. *Wisdom* is "the proper use (or application) of knowledge (information)." It's doing the right thing at the right time. My (Eddie) father was a wonderfully wise man. I remember two words of wisdom he gave me as a boy that exemplify this point.

> **"Get wisdom, get understanding."**

He said, "There are often wrong ways to do the right thing; but there is never a right way to do the wrong thing." He also taught me, "Doing the right thing at the wrong time makes it the wrong thing." King Solomon, the world's wisest man, encouraged us in Proverbs 4:5, *"Get wisdom, get understanding."*

An impartation of wisdom can be the turning point in our lives. Those with years of experience can be a source of wisdom. We can save ourselves years of fruitless effort by implementing a timely word from the wise, or by following their system. Surround yourself with the right books and with people who are wiser than you. Most importantly, *ask for it*. James 1:5, NIV says, *"If any of you lacks wisdom, he should ask God, who gives generously to all without finding fault, and it will be given to him."* Whatever you do, *get wisdom*.

Intuition

Another source of invaluable information comes from the inner voice within. Each of us has an inner voice. We call it *intuition*. Intuition is that quick insight that we get from our subconscious minds when we are consciously making decisions or doing research. Some call it "a gut feeling." We Christians know it as that *"still, small voice,"* mentioned in 1 Kings 19:11-12. The Psalmist advised us to *"be still, and know."* (Psalms 46:10)

When we are born again, God's Holy Spirit comes into our hearts and becomes one with our spirits. He will speak to us, but we must learn to be still and to hear His voice. Many of us are too focused on the big, the external influences around us. We so look for life's *suddenlies* that we miss life's *subtleties*. It's easy in our busy, fast-paced lives for us to overlook the inner voice that tells us, "Look at things *this* way;" or simply provides a mental "yes" or "no" to our queries.

It's often difficult to differentiate between *our* inner voice, *the Holy Spirit's* voice within us, and *the voice of the enemy.* When we experience an intuitive download, we should filter it through wisdom, godly counsel, and the Word of God. God will never say something in our hearts that is contrary to the Bible—His written Word. These help us to avoid deception and stay on course.

Research

Once we've identified our sources of wisdom and gathered our information, then we need to review the information gathered. Remember, *to research* means to "investigate diligently." The word *investigate* comes from the root "in footsteps." When we investigate, we in effect retrace the steps of those who've gone before us. We incorporate their successful results into our stories.

We were told, and perhaps you were told as well, that we should learn from our failures. We should certainly learn from our failures. However, it's wiser still to learn from the mistakes of others. There is no need for us to repeat their failures.

As we research, we are inspired by the testimonies of successful people as we discover how they overcame failure time after time. We should keep an open mind and think outside the box when we research for our goals. Our investigation will always produce something new, fresh, and exciting.

> **Don't succumb to analysis paralysis.**

Research is important. But let's not get bogged down in our research. Otherwise we will yield to inaction, procrastination, and it could possibly cost us our lives. Imagine how many lives could have been saved if the newest treatment for AIDS and cancer hadn't been delayed by bureaucratic red tape. Let's not succumb to *analysis paralysis*.

Windows of Opportunity

I (Kenn) remember when the real estate bubble began in California and elsewhere in 2003 and 2004. As a result of my market research I knew that there was a good chance that a correction in those markets would occur soon. I also noticed through research and my personal experience that other areas of the nation were experiencing different real estate cycles. Central Texas, for example, was on a counter cycle to the coasts.

I presented scores of seminars across the nation where I informed property owners to get their over-inflated real estate equity out to safer havens like Texas, which was on a counter cycle. I also knew that there was a limited time for them to take action—a window of opportunity was closing.

Many did as I suggested. However, many more people later wished they had taken my advice and moved their equity to safer havens prior to seeing it evaporate in the real estate correction of 2007 and 2008. As has been said, "he who hesitates is lost."

Here then is the formula:

Research + wisdom + action = success.

Now go to page 126 to complete this chapter's Action Exercise.

Identify Who'll Help
Identify Those to Avoid
Advocacy

Chapter 10
Step Nine – Advocates

Identify Those Who'll Help / Identify Those to Avoid / Advocacy

"But the advocate the Holy Spirit, whom the Father will send in my name, will teach you all things..."
(John 14:26)

Identify Those Who'll Help

To reach our goals we each need help. We can't do it alone. The question is, "Where do we find help?" The Bible provides part of the answer in Luke 6:38, where Jesus said, *"Give, and it shall be given unto you..."* Every time we help someone get what he or she wants or needs we *plant a seed.* In time, that seed will produce fruit, and someone will help us get what we want or need. According to late great Christian business trainer Zig Ziglar, *"You can have everything in life you want if you will just help enough other people get what they want."*

In our goals journals we list the people who can, and may be willing to help us achieve our goals. They could be our spouses, our boss', our past clients, friends, trusted advisors, or our coaches. What we're looking for are trustworthy people who have our best interests in mind. We're looking for other goal-oriented individuals who will encourage and support us when the challenges come—and they will.

I (Kenn) co-founded a group called the *Inner Circle Business Network,* a group of goal-oriented professionals who meet once a month to network, and to share success ideas. We determined that there are wheels of relationships like a series of concentric circles. One of our primary goals is to bring more people who are in our "network of support circles" closer to our "inner circles."

Consider your business network group. The outer circle of your group starts with 5,000 or more people, or those we call *everybodys*—people who only know *of* you.

The next circle, somewhat smaller, consists of your *acquaintances* or 500 (more or less) people who *know of* you, and who *know what you do.*

| **Who knows, likes, and trusts you?** |

The next smaller circle consists of 70 or fewer people who *know* you, who *know what you do,* and who *will refer your services.* In marketing lingo, we'd say that *they know, like, and trust you.*

Then there is your *inner circle,* "your 12." These are your closest associates, on whom you can *always* depend. They will defend you at all costs. We call them our *advocates,* those we with whom we are "in relationship." They are doing life together with us.

Finally, there is your *inner-inner circle*, the two or three people who are closest to you. We refer to it as the "three foot rule." These individuals are within arm's length of you. You lock shields with them and they with you. As my former Inner Circle friend, the late Kenton Brown would say, "These are the people who would come and bail you out of a Mexican jail at 3 o'clock in the morning." Very few people are a fit for your *inner-inner circle*. Choose your *inner-inner circle* members wisely.

These concentric circles are a loose depiction of the life of Christ. He had the thousands who knew of Him. One example was the 5,000 that He fed with the loaves and fish. There were the 70 that He sent out two-by-two on a ministry assignment. Then there were Jesus' chosen 12 disciples. But only three of them, Peter, James and John were His closest confidants. They were His *inner-inner circle*. We are to love everybody. However, we are not to confide in everybody. We need to identify those we know and those who we would like to know who can help push us towards our goals.

In your goals journal, write down 12 people *you know personally* who could help you reach your goal. Then write down 12 people who *you would like to meet* who might possibly help you reach your goal. The key about your "would like to meet" list is not to limit yourself. Over time we have met many of our heroes who we never thought we'd meet personally. They were on our "lists." Some of them have become our close personal mentors and advisors. Frankly, it astonishes us still. We are blessed.

Identify Those to Avoid

Not to sound negative but it is important for us to list those people we need to avoid. It is inevitable that we will get resistance to our new ideas or ventures from some people. It's part of the process. After all, as we've pointed out, only three percent of the world's population has written out their goals. So, ninety-seven percent of your friends may not share your passion to achieve.

Although some of your friends will support your goals, many "well meaning" people, even close friends and family members may not share your dream. And sad to say, there are some who are actually caustic to goal achievement. You need to keep at a distance negative, pessimistic people if you're to succeed.

At times Jesus' closest followers didn't understand His priorities. We find one example in John 7:1-8 (The Message) where we read:

> *Later Jesus was going about his business in Galilee. He didn't want to travel in Judea because the Jews there were looking for a chance to kill him. It was near the time of Tabernacles, a feast observed annually by the Jews.*
>
> [3-5] *His brothers said, "Why don't you leave here and go up to the Feast so your disciples can get a good look at the works you do? No one who intends to be publicly known does everything behind the scenes. If you're serious about what you are doing, come out in the open and show the world." His brothers were pushing him like this because they didn't believe in him either.*

6-8 Jesus came back at them, "Don't crowd me. This isn't my time. It's your time—it's always your time; you have nothing to lose. The world has nothing against you, but it's up in arms against me. It's against me because I expose the evil behind its pretensions. You go ahead, go up to the Feast. Don't wait for me. I'm not ready. It's not the right time for me."

Another group to beware of is the news media—radio, television, Internet and print newscasters who report bad news story after bad news story. You say—how will I stay informed if I don't watch, listen to, or read the daily news? You shouldn't worry about that. When it comes to the "talking heads" on TV, much of their information contains more opinion and political spin than truth. Why is this? It's simple. The reason is ratings. Bad news sells better than good news. It's amazing how they can turn good news into bad news. News, especially bad news, can be toxic to your goal achievement.

> **Never rent space in your brain to negative news!**

My wife (Kenn's wife Michele) never watches the news and she is happier and more fulfilled staying away from the "ain't it awful" broadcasts. I remember talking to her about an air crash in the Potomac River about three weeks after the event. Although it had a heroic ending, my wife was totally unaware of the disaster. I realized that she hadn't needed to know about that story. It had no impact on her life whatsoever. Negative news doesn't "take up space" in her brain.

Long ago I learned to generally *keep my goals secret*. That way the "nay sayers" won't have a chance to help me change my mind. The exceptions to the rule are:

1. Other goal-oriented individuals
2. Advocates who will help you get there

Only share your dreams with those who you know, like, and trust; and who know the power of goal setting. Surround yourself with positive, up-beat, goal-oriented team players. Avoid negative, energy draining, depressing, unmotivated, non-goal-oriented people. They will only drag you down.

Advocacy

"Stand By Me" – Performed by Ben E. King

When striving to reach our goals, we need to *associate* with *advocates*. *Advocate* is a legal term, which means "one who comes alongside." An advocate is someone you call in time of need.

In John, Chapters 15 and 16, Jesus announced that upon His ascension into heaven His *advocate* would appear. Depending on which version of the Bible you are reading the Holy Spirit is referred to as "comforter," "counselor," or "advocate." It's actually translated from the Greek word "paraclete." The role of the Holy Spirit is largely to serve as an attorney for Christ. We could say that He pleads Christ's case to men, to convince them that Jesus is Messiah.

An *advocate* then is someone who will defend you and speak fervently in favor of you. A person who will come to your side, defend, promote, encourage, edify, and exhort you. It's important that you both find your advocates; and be an advocate. Who can you call on at any time, personally and/or professionally, who will come to your side in good times or bad? And who are *you* willing to jump up and defend or promote anytime, anywhere?

T.E.A.M.

In business I (Kenn) teach my clients that they need a team of advisors and advocates. I use the acronym T.E.A.M.—**T**rusted **E**xperts, **A**dvisors, and **M**entors. Each of us needs to develop a team of people who will help us meet our goals.

It isn't difficult to develop a team. Start with the professionals you already admire and ask them who they depend on for advice. Then seek to engage those individuals. The most successful professionals have a network of advocates and advisors. Contact them and ask to become part of their networks.

Advocates outside of the business arena are equally important. These could include your friends or a family member. My (Kenn's) father-in-law is an advocate to my kids because he will drop most anything to come to their side when they call on him. He defends their causes at times even when they are wrong. He is committed to them; on their side and by their side. Their granddaddy is definitely their *advocate*.

As we close this chapter, remember that you have "a heavenly Advocate," Jesus Christ. John reminds us in 1 John 2:1-2 that He, like a divine defense attorney, is in heaven ready to defend us when we sin. As Hebrews 7:25 says, Jesus intercedes (advocates) for us there once we receive Him as our Savior. He personally paid the price for our sin. (See Appendix A on page 132).

Now complete the Action Exercise on page 128.

www.MaximumDreamAchievement.com

Make a Plan
Take Action
Activation

Chapter 11
Step Ten – Plan

Make a Plan / Take Action / Activation

"Therefore go"
(Matt 28:19)

Make a Plan

> "He, who fails to plan, plans to fail."

Each of us needs a written plan of action. Just as every successful product or mission needs a plan of action, so each goal-achieving journey needs a plan of action. It needs a series of activities that are to be accomplished in an established order. A purposeful plan of action is a written order of activities—steps to be followed. First do *this*; next, do *that*. If our plan is poorly written or executed, chances are we will fail. As the saying goes, "He, who fails to plan, plans to fail."

Think of building of a house. The plans are established before the actual building begins. Plans need to be specific and in proper order. Consider the architect's blueprint used to build a building. The blueprint is a detailed schematic of the proposed structure to be built.

First there is a rough sketch. Then the architect adds the details as he or she creates the builder's blueprints. Not a nail is driven or a brick laid without the completed blueprint—the necessary visual plans. The builders don't start with plumbing and electrical. They first clear the lot, do the utility work, set the foundation, etc. In fact, there are over 250,000 steps in the construction of a new house; each of which must be done in a very specific order.

Before you begin the journey to reach your goal, you need a written plan. If you don't know how to create one, find someone who does and ask him or her to help you. Plans can include a schematic or flow chart showing how these activities fit together. I (Kenn) have written step-by-step plans of action that govern my priorities and order my activities. I am also a visual person. So I like to put my plans of action into a flow chart or "mind map." We recommend a free, downloadable mind mapping software that you can find on the Internet, called "FreeMind."

Suppose your goal is to start a new business. If so, then you'll need a detailed written business plan. You must know why and how your business will run, and what its clear objectives are. You will want to describe in writing the service or product your business will provide, and the problems it will solve.

Poor planning and poor leadership are the top two reasons that most businesses fail in their first year. A well thought out, proven business model is why franchises have a much better rate of success than mom and pop shops. Again, if you're unsure about how to put together a plan—recruit someone who knows how to help you with your business plan. Google *business plan, templates*. I (Eddie) just did and found 28 million results. (Also try *business plan outline*)

There are courses we can take on business planning. If you are going to take a course, make sure it is from someone who has been successful. Don't waste your time learning theory from an unproven teacher. Seek wise counsel from successful people because success begets success. In Proverbs 11:14 we learn that there is value in having a multitude of counselors.

Advance planning saves time

When as a Realtor I (Kenn) sell a home, at my first meeting with the buyer I help them develop a plan for home ownership. I provide them with a book I have written on home ownership, entitled: *Home Buying Secrets Revealed*. (Available at: http://HomeBuyingSecretsRevealed.com)

Then I go over the 10 steps to buying a home. I have them write their *needs and wants list*. We discuss timing and financing. At that point, I help them create a plan before we ever step into the car to go look at homes. This helps them and me stay on track. We can certainly revise the plan as we go, but ultimately we know what we are shooting for.

When I talk with business leaders about a new venture they invariably ask, "What's the vision? What's the plan?" The plan doesn't have to be perfect or fully complete at first; but it does need to be solid, well thought out, and have a definite objective.

When you've completed your plan, ask several trusted advisors and advocates to review it. They will each see your plan from a different angle and their feedback will help to fill in the gaps.

Priorities

Time management is the art of putting our primary activities on a calendar and being disciplined to perform them at the appointed time. We call this *Time Blocking*, which is crucial to goal achievement. Focused time management accelerates us toward our preferred future. It helps keep us on target and holds us accountable to our schedules. To Time Block we need a weekly calendar on which we can block hours of time during which we will do certain activities. We like to do this ahead of time so we can keep our weekly activities on track.

Some rules about time management:

1. Time Block your personal, family, free, and devotional time first.
2. Time Block your weekly primary income producing activities and ruthlessly guard those times.
3. Concentrate on the twenty percent of your activities that will provide eighty percent of your results.
4. Set your calendar and others will line up behind you.
5. Learn how to politely yet firmly say "no" to activities that will take you off track. To say "no" to one thing is in effect to say "yes" to another.
6. Learn to do what is right. Doing good things may not necessarily be the *right* thing. Doing the

right thing at the right time is always a good thing.

7. What you erase, you must replace. If an unexpected event causes you to miss a primary activity, find another time on your calendar to replace the time you missed.

Take the First Step

I (Kenn) learned a long time ago how huge it is to take the first step to launch a new goal. I was at a friend's book signing and there were several people in attendance who wanted to write books. I challenged them to go home and write the first line. Write the first page. Many of them emailed me and said it was that call to action that got them moving. Try it. To simply write one sentence often "primes the pump."

My coauthor, Eddie Smith, is also an author as well as a writing coach. He says that the hardest thing for him to do is to sit down and *start to write*; but that the second hardest thing for him to do is to *stop writing* once he starts.

There is something powerful about taking that initial action toward your goal. It is like the simple act of turning the ignition in your car. You can't go anywhere until you first turn the key. Once you do, then you are free to move about the countryside. So take that first action at the appointed time, which may be *right now*.

> **Procrastination is a dream killer.**

Now is better than later. *Now* has power and creates momentum. So if you haven't written down your goals, do it today. Use your goals journal and *start today*. Busyness is a modern plague. Do not succumb to all the other voices calling for your attention.

What will it be? Today? Someday? Or will it be never? A respected author once told me that the wealthiest place on earth is the cemetery. Why? Because the cemetery is filled with books, songs, businesses, etc. that could have been created, but never were. Those were buried with the deceased.

I (Eddie) often challenge people, "Don't take your book to heaven." Don't procrastinate. Do that for which you were created. Don't be like those who bury their dreams and aspirations. You are blessed to be a blessing. Make a plan and get started; and if possible, start today!

Taking Your Goal Into an Action Plan

We've learned that to achieve any big goal one must establish a series of small goals. Or as is sometimes said, "The best way to eat an elephant is one bite at a time." Maybe your three-year goal is to triple your income, or to lose twenty pounds. Divide the goal by three and that will tell you how much you will have to work each year to meet your goal.

For instance, if you currently make $3,000 per month and you want to make $9,000 per month, you'll need to increase your income producing activities to make an additional $2,000 per month by year-end. Then by the end of the second year, increase your income another $2,000 per month, and by year three, another $2,000 per month. This will put you at the $9,000 income figure.

Now take the additional $2,000 per month and break it down by week. There are roughly four weeks in a month, which equates to $500 per week. What income producing activities will you have to do to make an extra $500 per week? I can think of a few. One might be to wake up an hour or two earlier each day. Another may be to add a second job, do network marketing, or better yet, get more productive at your current job so you can get a raise (or all of the above).

Suppose your goal is weight loss. To lose twenty pounds over 36 months is a little over half a pound per month or one-eighth of a pound per week. How much more exercise will be required, and what kind of foods will you have to cut out of your diet to lose that one-eighth of a pound per week? What must you add to, or cut from your daily routine to meet your goal?

Goal achievement isn't as much about doing as it is about *becoming*. What kind of person will you have to become if you're to reach your goal? Your "big how" is reached by a series of "little hows." So once you decide to reach your big dream, break it down into smaller goals. Then apply the activities that will be necessary for you to add to your weekly and daily plan of action.

We start with the end goal in mind. Then we back out our timeline from the end to the beginning. I (Kenn) spread my to-do lists in columns where I can categorize my activities based on the time required for their completion.

Think about your projects the way you might plan an event. Work backwards from the *event date*. Break down yours according to what you must do over specific periods of time.

Activation

We love the multiple definitions for the word "activation." They are both descriptive and motivating. To have a goal backed by a solid plan of action, and then to get started is a recipe for success. Once you have this recipe, then light the fire and get cookin'. In other words, *activate* your goal.

Webster's Dictionary defines the word *activate* as to "set in motion." It's similar to firing a starting gun at the beginning of a race. It gets everyone moving.

To *activate* is also a military term, which means "to gather and organize the troops for a mission." When you activate you will be surprised to see how your crew, your cohorts, and your staff get moving.

Activation can also mean, "to mix with oxygen." Newer automobiles today employ fuel injectors; while older cars have carburetors that mix the gasoline fuel with oxygen. Why is that? It is because cars don't actually burn liquid gasoline. They burn a mixture of oxygenated gasoline fumes. In the same manner, we become inspired when we breathe life into our dreams and goals. *Inspiration is fuel.*

Activation is also a term used to describe "purification." A fountain running in a pond of water is not there just for beauty. It activates and purifies the pond by agitating and adding life-giving oxygen to the water.

When you experience stagnant seasons in your life, which we all do at times, you may need some fresh inspiration and purification. Perhaps you need to rid yourself of some things that distract you from focusing on your goal.

Activation also means, "to accelerate a reaction as with heat." When you start the fire beneath that pot of water, it is relatively calm. However, after about ten minutes on high heat and it is activated into a roiling boil. For us, it all begins when we take that first action and light the fire under our goals.

In science, to *activate a substance* is to make it radioactive. Part of the process in making an atomic bomb includes turning water into heavy water through a process called *activation*. In goal setting, when activated, our dreams and goals can, like a nuclear chain reaction, release a massive blast of energy. Do you want an explosive release of positive energy? We do! Then get ready, get set—*get activated*!

This chapter's Action Exercise is on page 130.

www.MaximumDreamAchievement.com

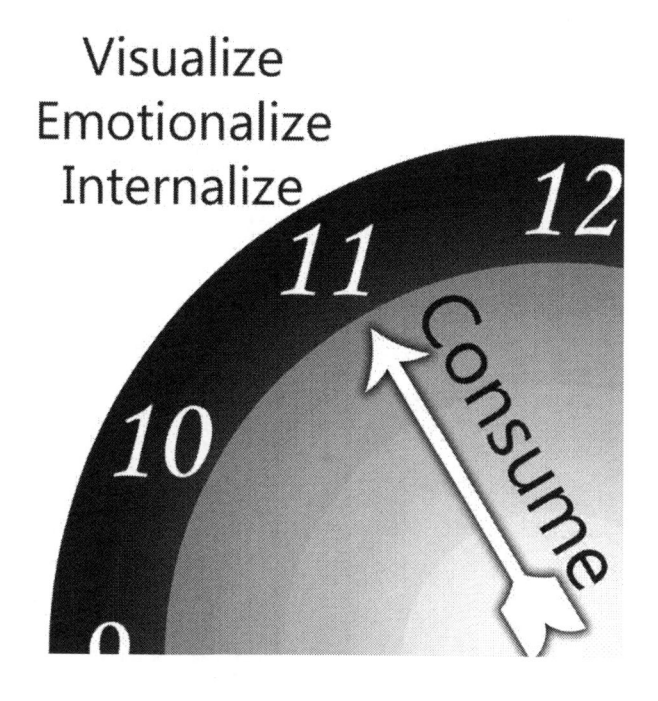

Chapter 12
Step Eleven – Consume

Visualize / Emotionalize / Internalize

"I was blind but now I see"
(John 9:25)

Visualize

To "visualize" is to *meditate,* to see an outcome in your mind's eye. Unfortunately, some people understand visualization only in terms of new age mysticism. The truth is, visualization is quite biblical. Jesus taught, *"Therefore I tell you, whatever you ask for in prayer, believe that you have received it, and it will be yours"* (Mark 11:24). For us to believe that we *have received* what we are praying for is to visualize it as already accomplished!

The Psalmist referred to his speech and visualization when he prayed, *"May the words of my mouth and the meditation of my heart* (visualization) *be pleasing in your sight, O LORD, my Rock and my Redeemer"* (Psalm 19:14). And, the Apostle Paul taught us to pray without anxiety and with thanksgiving in Philippians 4:6. What is that? It's not to look at things the way they are, but instead to visualize them the way we expect them to be when God has heard and answered us.

Many professional athletes invest much of their training time to meditation, or visualization. The basketball player sees himself shoot the ball and the ball going through the hoop in his mind's eye as he meditates. The tennis player mentally sees himself return the serve successfully. They do this over and over again. So visualization has many powerful applications. Since it's this powerful, let's apply it to achieving our goals. How?

> **To make a habit of routinely visualizing our goals as completed will keep the wind in our sails.**

Find a quiet place that is free from distraction where you can close your eyes and *visualize* your goal—as already completed. Just as the successful athletes who do it, you too will find this both inspiring and motivating. To make a habit of routinely visualizing our goals as accomplished will keep the wind in our sails.

That's right. For us to consistently visualize our preferred futures is important because there are a great many visuals competing for our attention. We want *our* visuals to be at the forefront of our consciousness, not those created by clever marketers. Advertisers know this strategy all too well. Here is an example.

Last night as I (Kenn) watched television, it seemed like every commercial was of hot, steamy pizza. The visual of the crispy crust, the melting cheese and the fragrant pepperoni was so compelling I could almost smell the pizza. Yep, you guessed it. Before the show was over there was a pizza in our oven! Those visuals prompted me to get up and take action!

Let's keep the visuals of our dreams constantly in minds. Let's *visualize* our goals as fully accomplished! When it's all said and done, either we will control the visuals that parade across our minds or someone else will. Let's become *destiny visionaries*.

Many years ago a motivational trainer came to my office and told me (Kenn) to find a picture (perhaps in a magazine) that would represent one of my goals—such as a dream vacation or a fancy car. I was to cut it out and glue a photo of myself into the photo. Then I was to keep it in a place where I would see it daily. These are called *dream boards* or *vision boards*. It worked!

The photo that I selected was of Ka'anapali Beach in Maui. I put a photo of my future wife and myself in the picture and sure enough within one year we were on that very beach!

We experienced the same amazing power of visualization later when we planned our dream home. I sketched the downstairs and upstairs of my dream home. Although my wife isn't an artist, she could "see" her dream house in her mind's eye.

She described a living room overlooking a pool with a beautiful lake view below. Less than four years after drawing and dreaming we found that very home. Or should I say—the home found us.

Seemingly out of the blue a division president for a large homebuilder called me. We talked shop for a while until he mentioned his new house was near completion. I asked what he was going to do with his old house. He said that he was going to put it on the market but not until he moved into his new one.

He described his current home to me and I said, "That sounds like a property we may be interested in." Amazingly, it was nearly the exact description of what my wife and I had visualized years before. Specifically—the downstairs was almost precisely what I had sketched. And yes, it has a pool and gorgeous lake view. *If we had never visualized it, we may not have recognized it or worse; failed to take advantage of the opportunity when it arrived.* The funny thing is that the home was never offered for sale on the open market.

AN IMPORTANT NOTE: New age mysticism gets off track when it assumes that *visualization IS the power.* It omits God altogether! We believe that God provides and that *visualization* helped to magnify our faith, and to cultivate our minds to recognize God's provision when it arrived! Remember, without faith we can't possibly please God. (Hebrews 11:6)

Emotionalize

Earlier we pointed out that people do what they do, and buy what they buy because of how it *makes them feel*. Most of what we do is in an attempt to avoid pain, or to experience pleasure. When we coach people regarding their goals, we ask them four questions:

1. What do you want?
2. Why do you want it?
3. What will it do for you (and others)?
4. How will it make you *feel*?

Suppose your goal is to open an orphanage in Costa Rica. Were you to reach that goal, you would experience certain feelings. What might they be? At some point you might be heard to say, "Wow, I feel great. Several dozen children now have food, clothing, shelter, education, and a brighter future because my goal has been accomplished. What a good feeling." We can't "think ourselves" to success. The ultimate driving factor in our lives is *how we feel* about succeeding.

If when growing up you continually heard "You won't amount to anything" or "money is the root of all evil," you may have been improperly programmed with negative and inaccurate information. (For the record, *money* is not the root of evil. It is the *love of money* according to 1 Timothy 6:10, which is the root of all kinds of evil.)

You may have to "clear the hard drive" of your mind, reformat, and reboot your thinking to some degree. We all have a common desire to be happy, healthy, and prosperous. No one wants to be depressed, unhealthy, and broke. But poor mental programming will keep us there.

Unfortunately, many people live mediocre lives due self-limiting emotional baggage from their past. Old, negative baggage needs to be dumped. If you feel you need help, seek pastoral counseling. Don't let past hang-ups keep you from moving forward.

> **Complaining is like a garbage magnet.**

Since most of our choices are determined by how we feel, we would do well to begin to associate positive feelings to the priorities that will move us toward our objective, and attach negative feelings to things that would hold us back or sidetrack us. Let's not become negative people, but rather abandon any negative mindset or activity like *complaining*. Complaining is like a garbage magnet. Time after time in the Old Testament we see how the Children of Israel missed out on God's best because they murmured and complained. Complaining never makes anything better.

The heart of the problem is the problem of the heart. And *emotionalizing* is a heart phenomenon. When we attach wonderful feelings to our dream (our preferred outcome), we create anticipation, excitement, and drive. We can certainly set the stage by listening to positive, upbeat music; watching encouraging videos; by listening to good motivational programs; and reading the Word of God. Positive daily affirmations also help maintain a positive emotional base.

Continue to report the good results that come your way. Celebrate them, even the smallest of them. No matter the circumstance, apply positive affirmations. Phrase them in short sentences you can repeat over and over. I (Kenn) add a little rhyme to my affirmations like "I am happy and healthy in every way, I am getting better and better each day."

Again, the power isn't in these things. The power is of God. These things simply "set the stage" for God to perform! Jesus said, *"Seek the Kingdom of God above all else, and live righteously, and he will give you everything you need"* (Matthew 6:33 NLT)

Paul, the Apostle, wrote in Philippians 4:8, *"Whatever is true, whatever is noble, whatever is right, whatever is pure, whatever is lovely, whatever is admirable – if anything is excellent or praiseworthy – think about such things."*

Attach *love*, the deepest of all emotions, to your activities. "I love what I am doing and where I am going." I love helping others. We might emotionalize writing this book because we know it will help you and others.

> **Be a grateful overcomer and enjoy the journey!**

Gratitude is also a quality we should incorporate into our goals journey. Let's be thankful that we're moving toward a wonderful preferred future. Will we face setbacks and disappointments along the way? Absolutely. At those points, we get up and go again.

Adversity in life is provided for our training. Negative experiences should only serve to make us more grateful as we overcome them. After all, the measure of our tests is the measure of our testimonies. As some say, "Negative experiences will either make you bitter or they will make you better. The choice is yours." Be a grateful overcomer and enjoy the journey!

Let's emotionalize our goals as if they were achieved in the same way that we visualize them achieved. Go ahead, pause for a moment and imagine your goal as having been reached. *Now feel the experience.*

Internalize

> **Our goals will actually begin to propel us from deep within.**

Next we need to *internalize* our goals. This goes beyond *visualizing* and *emotionalizing* them. It's here that we allow our goal to become part of who we are—our identity.

We have set the stage by journaling and posting written reminders on 3x5 cards and *Post It Notes* around us to keep our goals in view. We are speaking them aloud; and visualizing them as completed. Now it's time to *internalize* our goals through meditation. We meditate on our goals. One definition of *meditation* is to "revolve around in one's mind." To meditate on something is to analyze it from different angles.

Consider a large diamond. Depending on your perspective (your point of view, which is a view from a point), you will see a color. From one angle you'll see blue radiating from the diamond. From another, slightly different angle, you'll see red, and so on. So it is with effective meditation.

When we meditate correctly, we will see different dimensions of our goals and how we can achieve them. We will identify new, never-considered-before-approaches as to how we can reach our goals.

What we suggest is quite practical. We're not talking about the weird, secluded mountaintop guru type of meditation sitting cross-legged on the floor and humming. We are talking about pondering, rotating our objective around in our mind's eye with an expectant, prayerful perspective.

I (Eddie) find that when I awaken in the mornings, before I put one foot on the floor, my priorities begin to surface in my mind. It's absolutely remarkable how many times I receive fresh insights, understanding and discernment in those times. Is it God speaking to me? Sometimes, I'm sure He is. Is it my subconscious mind, which submits solutions so freely because my conscious mind isn't so active yet? At times it is.

This is so powerful that I use it as a strategy. Here is an example. In writing my and my wife's book, *Spiritual Advocates* (Available at http://PrayerBookstore.com), we likened people who pray for others to defense attorneys, because they plead others' cases in prayer before Judge Jehovah (God) in heaven. As I began to write the chapter describing the Judge, I encountered a problem. What could I say about God (how could I describe Him) that would be fresh and insightful? He is omniscient, omnipresent, and omnipotent? Sure. But everyone has said that.

That night before I went to sleep I simply wrote out my question. "God how can I describe you in this book?" I put the question on my nightstand.

The next morning, as I awoke and before my conscious mind had kicked into gear, I listened. I meditated and pondered. At one point the phrase "fruit of the Spirit" came to mind. (Note: In life and in ministry to someone we often discount the first thing that comes to mind. Why? Because we don't think it could be that easy. Or, because what we receive makes very little sense to us at the moment as in this illustration.)

I didn't understand what "fruit of the Spirit" had to do with a description of God. But I faithfully recorded it in my journal.

Later that day I began to mediate again on the matter, *and I got it!* The "fruit of the Spirit," which are nine qualities Paul lists in Galatians 5:22-23 are the fruit or the evidence of God's presence in our lives. It's like a verbal photograph of God. He is a loving God, a joyful God, a peaceful God, and etc. And aren't we grateful that He is a patient God?

Hopefully you can see how that meditation strategy provided the structure for a fairly unique chapter in our book.

King David was certainly successful in business. Meditating was on his agenda. In Psalm 19:14 he prayed, *"May the words of my mouth and* the meditation *of my heart be pleasing in your sight, O LORD, my Rock and my Redeemer.*

As we meditate, our goals become *internalized*. They will become part of who we are. Our goals will then actually begin to propel us from deep within.

Mind, Heart, Gut

We mentally *visualize* our goal; we see it (and hear it). We *emotionalize* our goal; we feel it. Finally, we *internalize* our goal; and allow it to become part of who we are. Reaching our goal then becomes almost instinctual. When we align our mind,

www.MaximumDreamAchievement.com

heart, and our gut toward reaching our goals, we have created a condition and an atmosphere that will propel and sustain us toward our accomplishment.

Please go to page 132 and do the Action Exercise.

**Persistence
Patience
Prayer**

Chapter 13
Step Twelve – Power

Persistence / Patience / Prayer

"Your Kingdom come, your will be done"
(Matthew 6:10)

Persistence

Throughout our journey toward reaching our goal, we must remain *committed to it* and *persistently pursue it* until it comes to fruition. It's important that we maintain a "never give up" attitude and press in to see it completed.

> **We can only win if we stay in the game.**

Any worthwhile achievement will meet resistance, and *resistance requires persistence*. If achieving one's goal were easy everyone would do it. Remember, only three percent of the population even bothers to write down their goals. It does demand effort. There'll be periods of struggle and setback, as well as times of breakthrough. One thing is for certain—*we can only win if we stay in the game.*

Yes, it may harder and take you longer to reach your goal than you originally thought. But if you persevere, you will cross the finish line. I (Kenn) have never had a case where a client who really wanted to own a home could not get one as long as he or she did what was necessary and *persisted.*

I actually worked with one client for three years to get her into a home. Credit, divorce, and job issues all came into play. She is now a happy homeowner because neither she nor I ever gave up!

Unfortunately, I have had clients who did give up. They quit. I doubt that they are homeowners today and they may rent forever. But after thousands of transactions during my thirty years in real estate, all of my clients who persisted got their homes.

Persistence, which is a test of our faith, builds our character and confidence. It prepares us to push through the resistance during the truly tough times. It builds our strength to accomplish even greater challenges in the future. In fact the greater your goal is; the greater your need to be persistent.

Paul, the Apostle, in Philippians 3:13 said it this way. *"…One thing I do, forgetting what is behind and reaching forward to those things which are ahead,* I press toward the goal—*for the prize…"*

The root of the word *persistence* means, "to stand firm." Paul told the Christians in Corinth, *"Therefore, my dear brothers and sisters,* stand firm. Let nothing move you. *Always give yourselves fully to the work of the Lord, because you know that your labor in the Lord is not in vain"* (1 Corinthians 15:58).

Persistence was a big deal to Paul. He stressed it with the Ephesian Christians. Perhaps you remember this familiar passage: Ephesians 6:10-17

> "*¹⁰ Finally,* be strong *in the Lord and in his mighty power. ¹¹ Put on the full armor of God, so that you can* take your **stand** *against the devil's schemes. ¹² For our struggle is not against flesh and blood, but against the rulers, against the authorities, against the powers of this dark world and against the spiritual forces of evil in the heavenly realms. ¹³ Therefore put on the full armor of God, so that when the day of evil comes,* you may be able to **stand** *your ground, and after you have done everything, to* **stand**. *¹⁴* **Stand** *firm then, with the belt of truth buckled around your waist, with the breastplate of righteousness in place, ¹⁵ and with your feet fitted with the readiness that comes from the gospel of peace. ¹⁶ In addition to all this, take up the shield of faith, with which you can extinguish all the flaming arrows of the evil one. ¹⁷ Take the helmet of salvation and the sword of the Spirit, which is the word of God.*"

> **"If you must fall, *fall forward!*"**

If our goals are worthwhile, we must stand our ground! Too many people quit when the going gets tough. Don't be a quitter. You may have to take a detour along the way, but keep moving forward. My (Eddie) high school football coach stressed, "If you must fall, *fall forward!*" Friend, our encouragement to you today is that you *persist* and press on.

Patience

Ahhh..., *patience*. Now let's stop here. We, Kenn and Eddie, are both *Type A* personalities. Suffice it to say, we don't necessarily have a firm grasp on patience. Our wives will attest to that. We want our goals and we want them now! <smile>

Although we're certainly not the poster children of patience, over the years we have learned a measure of patience. Those who know us best would likely agree that we are more patient today than we were in years gone by. We are making progress.

Patience is crucial to our goal accomplishment journey. It helps us develop humility, and humility helps us build patience. If we could have everything we want right now—anything—we'd become spoiled brats and be diminished by it. Our drive to succeed would be compromised. So, we are learning to slow down and smell the flowers along the way.

Learning patience helps us on our journey as well as with our relationships. Do you feel uncomfortable standing in a grocery line with an impatient person? We understand. We used to be the guys in line who tapped their toes, looked at their watches, and offered the heavy impatient sighs.

At one point, we've each lived in California. It wasn't until we arrived on the West Coast that we learned how slowly things move in Texas. Cars out there travel 90 miles per hour on the freeway. The Starbucks lines moves quicker. People neither take the time to smell the coffee nor the roses! You just might get pushed in line from behind, or pushed off the freeway by a Porsche or a soccer mom in a minivan.

At this point we're both Texans. Texas culture is more friendly, easy going, and talkative. Sure, we wait longer in line, and our traffic moves a little slower. Patient people do take time to smell flowers. They're not uptight. They are more childlike.

Jesus loved children. He drew them to himself and used them as illustrations of what citizens of heaven are like. In Mark 10:15 He said, *"Truly I tell you, anyone who will not receive the kingdom of God like a little child will never enter it."* Understand that the value is being *childlike,* and not *childish.* Childishness is simple immaturity.

Honestly, every goal we have ever set has taken us longer and cost us more, in terms of effort and resources, than we first considered. It was *patience* and *persistence* that pulled us through. To prevent disappointment and discouragement, we must develop patience. The question is: *how?* Where does one find patience?

The Apostle Paul, who is like our life coach, tells us in Galatians 5:22a. He says, *"But the Spirit produces…patience… and self-control."* Patience is evidence that we are filled with God's Holy Spirit.

> **A person without patience is a person without peace.**

Patience will provide peace during life's inevitable setbacks. Paul said that this *"peace…which surpasses all understanding* will guard your hearts and minds…" (Philippians 4:7).

Peace, another fruit of the Holy Spirit, will guard and protect us. *Patience* provides a peaceful, confident expectation that our preferred future will come to pass. A person without patience is a person without peace. "Patience is a virtue." Interestingly, no one knows for sure the source of this familiar, and one of the truest quotes of all time. Patience, when tied together with persistence creates an incredible force in our lives.

Prayer

As we come to the final section of our book, we congratulate you for making it this far. It's well-known in the publishing industry that the majority of the books that people start to read are never finished. We understand. Both of us have unfinished books in our libraries. We either lost interest while reading them; or another more interesting book came along; or our wives decided they wanted to read the books we were reading and we don't know where they've hidden them!

So again, thank you for your persistence in staying with us to this point. You'll be glad you did. We are about to discuss perhaps the most important section of this book. We consider it the ultimate key that unlocks the power of goals. It's been both the catalyst and sustainer during our goals journeys. Are you ready? Here it is!

> **It's about our prayers being answered and our dreams being realized.**

The secret to virtually every truly great achievement throughout history has been *the power of prayer*. It's profoundly simple; yet simply profound. Realize, we aren't referring to religion. Religion has never helped anyone. We're referring to a vital, living relationship with our Creator God. Prayer, our connection with Him, is the key to ultimate success. There is an old song that says, "Prayer is the key to heaven; but faith unlocks the door." It's about our prayers being heard and answered, and our dreams being realized.

NOTE: Before we travel any further allow us to ask you this important question. "Do you have a genuine, vital, living relationship with your Creator God through His Son, Jesus Christ?" Another way to ask it is: "If you were to die today, do you have the assurance in your heart that you would go to heaven?" If not, we encourage you to bookmark this page and spend a few minutes reading and processing the section entitled, *Appendix A*, in the back of this book. We've placed it there expressly to share with you the abundant and eternal life we've each received through Christ!

We are firm believers in the power of prayer when it comes to goal achievement. That belief comes from seeing God's answers to our prayers. As has been said, "A man with an experience is never at the mercy of a man with an argument." <smile> We have each experienced the awesome power of answered prayer. As a result of prayer, God has fulfilled many of our desires and dreams.

I (Eddie) was being interviewed on a radio talk show about my book, *How To Be Heard in Heaven* (Available at http://PrayerBookstore.com) when I mentioned this issue of answered prayer. The host said, "Do you mean that you can identify something that God did in direct response to your prayer?"

I replied, "Yes, indeed. Why would I spend a moment in prayer if I had no evidence or faith that God would answer? I can show you many direct answers to prayer."

She said, "Eddie, I've been a Christian for 20 years and I couldn't tell you any specific thing that I've seen God do in answer to my prayer. Could you give us an example?"

I began telling her a story of 27 gentlemen's clubs (certainly a misnomer for them), strip joints that were simultaneously shut down as a result of focused prayer.

"Wow!" She interrupted.

"Well I'm not through," I said as I told her how we had taken Christmas gifts to the ladies who worked in them, praying that we'd have an opportunity to make a difference in their lives; and how one of those exotic dancers answered my wife and my newspaper ad and came to rent our townhouse.

Again she interrupted. I said, "Well, I'm not finished."

I went on to tell her how my wife, Alice and I befriended her and her two precious preschool children over a period of a year and one-half, and saw her come to Christ.

She interrupted once more, and once more I said, "Well, I'm not finished yet."

I continued to tell her how the young lady returned to her father's house (a physician) and ultimately went to Oxford University in England.

She thanked me and I continued telling her how that lady is now married and living with her family in New Jersey.

Needless to say, my poor radio host received more of an answer than she'd bargained for. <smile>

It's so sad, and so unnecessary that so few Christians see so few answers to prayer. God is poised to respond to us like a good daddy ready to shower his children with gifts. It's important that we learn how to make the connection in such a way that he both hears and answers our prayer. This is not so we can get what we want; but so you won't miss the treasures he has stored up for us! Beyond that, it's so we can help him extend his kingdom throughout the earth. He has invited us to joint venture with him in the family business—his kingdom on earth as it is in heaven!

This book that you are reading is also a result of answered prayer. Listen to God's promise. In Psalms 37:3 the psalmist said: *"Trust in the LORD and do good…Take delight in the LORD, and he will give you the desires of your heart. Commit your way to the LORD; trust in him and he will do this."* Nothing could be clearer.

We both saturate our goal setting process with prayer. We told you at the beginning of this book that the first steps are to want, to decide, to desire, and to commit. But before any of that, we encourage you to pray. Soak your entire goal setting process in prayer, meditation, and reflection. And take time to listen. Prayer is to be a dialogue, not a monologue. Don't be surprised if God doesn't give you guidance on reaching your goals, or redirect you regarding them, during your prayer time.

Prayer is an old English word that means, "to make entreaty, or an earnest request." In jolly ole England, one might have said to his hoped for future father-in-law, *"I pray thee Sire. May I have thy daughter's hand in marriage?"* Today, when we pray, we pray to our Father in heaven, the Creator of the Universe. To the Intelligence behind all that exists—God!

"Why pray?" One might ask. "Doesn't God already know what we need?" We find the answer in James 4:2b, ESV, *"You do not have, because you do not ask."* It certainly doesn't take a rocket scientist to understand that, does it? In Matthew 7:7, NIV, Jesus said, *"Ask and it will be given to you; seek and you will find; knock and the door will be opened to you."*

We learned long ago that when we don't ask, we don't receive. Learn to speak out your desired result and to seek divine revelation from beyond your own time and space limitations. Besides, He loves the sound of your voice.

Of course, it's contrary to our natural minds to ask for something as if we have already been given it. Why is that? Inside us exists a measure of doubt that what we asked someone for, they may not give us. We don't truly feel we can trust them with the answer. Doubt is the absence of faith. And remember, without faith we can't please God. (Hebrews 11:6)

Here is the bottom line. Your Father God is the only one you can fully trust. He is the only one who will never fail you. We're told to *"trust in the Lord with ALL your heart and lean not on your own understanding; in all your ways acknowledge him and he will make your paths straight"* (Proverbs 3:5-6 NIV).

| "Believing is seeing!" |

Based on that understanding, Jesus said, *"Therefore I tell you, whatever you ask in prayer,* believe that <u>you have received</u> it, *and it will be yours."*

Again, we are to pray with the mindset of one who has already received that for which he or she is asking. It's past tense—already done. Remarkable!

Paul wrote in Philippians 4:6, *"Do not be anxious about anything,* (Don't worry) *but in every situation, by prayer and petition,* with thanksgiving, *present your requests to God."* To beg our heavenly Daddy for something would insult Him. *What about persistence in prayer?* One might ask. To pray with faith believing that you already have that for which you are asking and to actively thank God for it, requires incredible persistence.

We are to believe we *have* already received that for which we are asking; and be so committed to it that we actually thank Him in advance! Perhaps you've heard it said, "Seeing is believing." When it comes to prayer however, "Believing is seeing!"

When we pray, we thank God by faith that our goal is already achieved. Where? It is already achieved at its designated time in the future.

And don't forget, prayer is a dialogue, not a monologue. It's more than making requests. It's a conversation. God often speaks to us (in our hearts) as we pray. We often discover the solutions to problems or new directions in which to move that we hadn't previously considered.

Sometimes when I (Kenn) pray I get fresh ideas, a song, or a new vision. When we lift up our goals to our Father in prayer, we present them by faith to the invisible realm of the Spirit. We ask God to make the invisible visible, the intangible tangible—to make them earthly reality.

NOTE: Before anything existed, God existed. The spirit-realm preceded the physical-realm. Nothing was seen until God said, *"Let there be light"* (Genesis 1:3). That which we see came from that which we cannot see, which explains why prayer is so critical to success in life and business.

True prayer produces peace. It's an expression of our faith-walk. And peace comes to us in three remarkable stages. We first experience *peace WITH God*. Then we can know the amazing *peace OF God*. Beyond that, we are offered God's *PERFECT Peace!*

Before we knew Christ as our Lord and Savior we were God's enemies (Colossians 1:21). When He saved us, Christ came to live in us and we experienced true peace. *This is peace WITH God.*

According to Ephesians 2:14, *Jesus is our peace*. When we receive Him, we receive peace. In John 14:27 He said He was *giving us His peace*. What greater peace could anyone hope for? There is no greater gift! So we who have *peace WITH God* can also experience the *peace of God*.

What is the peace of God? It's a peace that *"surpasses all understanding."* (Philippians 4:7). However, to enjoy His peace we must watch our "mental diet." In the next verses (verses 8 and 9, The Message Version), Paul instructs us...

> *"Summing it all up, friends, I'd say you'll do best by* filling your minds and meditating on things true, noble, reputable, authentic, compelling, gracious—the best, not the worst; the beautiful, not the ugly; things to praise, not things to curse. *Put into practice what you learned from me, what you heard and saw and realized. Do that, and God, who makes everything work together, will work you into his most excellent harmonies."*

> **Ultimately, God has "veto power" over our goal setting.**

Finally, we can know *perfect peace!* How? We know perfect peace when we elevate Him, in our minds, above all else—yes, even above our goals.

Ultimately, God has "veto power" with regard to our goal setting. That's a benefit of His being our King! He can, and sometimes does, alter our goal selection. He shifts and shapes them as we focus on Him. He must always be foremost in our thinking. In Isaiah 26:3, *"You keep him in perfect peace whose mind is stayed on you, because he trusts in you."*

To experience prayer that brings direction and peace, pray from a *position of thanksgiving*. Gratitude is a powerful force. The powerful combination of prayer, thanksgiving and meditation will create an atmosphere of positive expectation (faith) and results. Sometimes a simple "thank you" will open doors of opportunity that otherwise would not have opened.

Gratitude, giving thanks, is ingrained in our nature. We love to give and receive thanks. So again, thank you for reading our book. We hope it will help you on this journey we call "life."

Our hope for you is that in your life filled with setting and achieving goals, you might experience *Maximum Dream Achievement*. Our prayer for you:

> "May your goals and dreams come true, and may you receive a life filled with love, joy, peace, health, and prosperity. May our Father abundantly bless you." As one of our favorite mentors, the late Christian statesman and business coach Zig Ziglar so often said: "We'll see you *over* the top!"

Now complete the final Action Exercise on page 133.

www.MaximumDreamAchievement.com

www.MaximumDreamAchievement.com

Action Exercises

Step One – Want (Desire / Decide / Commit)

Reflection

"Well done good and faithful servant"
-Jesus (Matt 25:23)

Make a list of goals that you have already accomplished. It is important that you recognize and gratefully remember your past successes:

_____
_____
_____
_____
_____

Of what accomplishments or endeavors are you thankful and proud?

_____
_____
_____
_____
_____

Who have you met or become in relationship with for which you are thankful?

_____
_____
_____

www.MaximumDreamAchievement.com

_____
_____

What **one** accomplishment or endeavor pleases you most?
_____
_____
_____
_____
_____

What events have had the most positive impact on you?
_____
_____
_____
_____
_____

If you had to do it over again, which of your experiences would you like to re-live again?
_____
_____
_____
_____
_____

Projection

"What do you want?"
-Jesus (John 1:30)

Now to get your creative ambition juices flowing, answer this question: If you were handed $3 million tax free dollars what would you do with your time? What activities would you pursue? How would your day look? Where would you live? What kind of car would you drive? With whom would you spend most of your time?

_____
_____
_____
_____
_____

If you had exactly one year to live, what would you do with your time? With whom would you spend time? What activities would you pursue?

_____
_____
_____
_____
_____

10-Minute Life Changing Goal Setting Exercise

"Ask and you will receive"
-Jesus (Matt 7:7)

Find a quiet place without distractions. Get a timer or stopwatch. Close your eyes and imagine that you have unlimited funds and you are free from any hindering responsibilities.

If you could have anything you want in the next three years, what would it be? Now list all things you want for yourself, for your family, your community, for your church. What income level would you like to achieve? What relationships would you want to have? What spiritual desires and goals would you like to meet? Remember, if there were no limitations. Take three minutes and make a list.

1. _____
2. _____
3. _____
4. _____
5. _____
6. _____
7. _____
8. _____
9. _____
10. _____
11. _____
12. _____
13. _____
14. _____
15. _____
16. _____
17. _____
18. _____
19. _____
20. _____

(If you have more than 20, keep going!)

Now circle the **three** items that if achieved would have the biggest positive impact on your life.

Out of those three, pick the one goal that would have the biggest impact on your life.

This is the goal that we are going to use throughout the action exercises in this book.

You will be amazed that two-thirds of your three year written goals will be accomplished in the first twelve to eighteen months. You have begun the journey. Now let's go to work.

www.MaximumDreamAchievement.com

Step Two – Know
(Believe / Faith / Know)

"Everything is possible for one who believes"
-Jesus (Mark 9:236)

From Step One's goal exercise, take your primary goal (and the others when you are ready). Put your left index finger on that number one goal and your right hand on your forehead and say, "I have this" or "I am this" and follow with "so be it." In so doing, you are speaking against the unconscious mental doubts that would sabotage you and your future; and affirming your commitment to the process.

Say I believe (Your Goal) to be true—so be it. Now move your right hand to your heart and speak these words to the Father, "Lord, thank you for this. So be it." Then to your stomach and pray, "Lord, I gratefully receive and celebrate it."

Step Three - Ink
(Write It / Speak It / Proclaim It)

"I am who I am"
(Exod 3:14)

Take your important goals from the Step One exercise and fill in these sentences – put the goal in present tense (as completed):

I am _____
               (Identity / Existence)

Because _____
               (Reason / Cause)

So that _____
               (Results / Effect)

Example: I am earning twenty thousand per month every month by June
Because I have children going to college and I want a nicer home
So I am comfortably providing for my family's security and college education.

Repeat this exercise with all your important goals and keep them in your goals journal. Put the statements in a place you can see them each day. Consider sticky notes on your bathroom mirror and/or the visor of your car, 3x5 index cards in your pocket, or a white board at your office.

Step Four – Motives
(List Benefits / List Consequences / Motivations)

"For the joy set before him"
(Heb 12:2)

List ten to twenty benefits you or others will likely enjoy when you reach your goal. The first ten will be easy. It will get more difficult as you get to twenty. Push through—*the more benefits you see, the more motivated you will be.*

1. _____
2. _____
3. _____
4. _____
5. _____
6. _____
7. _____
8. _____
9. _____
10. _____
11. _____
12. _____
13. _____
14. _____
15. _____
16. _____
17. _____
18. _____
19. _____
20. _____

List at least five serious consequences that will result if you fail to reach your goal. Be real. These may be your catalyst for change.

1. _____
2. _____
3. _____
4. _____
5. _____

Anchoring Exercise

(Explanation: Without going into a long explanation, anchoring is a scientific term given to a way our minds and bodies relate. God has created us as complex beings. You may be familiar with cellular memory in which an amputee (who loses an arm) will still feel the itching of the arm they have lost.) Weird, huh? We are spirit, soul and body, and the connections between them are still being studied. So, anchoring is a proven psychological technique to help us make and keep our commitments. Consider it a memory aid. Here is an anchoring exercise.)

Now close your eyes, think of your goal, and open your hands as if to receive a gift. Say, "I receive the benefits of my goal achieved."

Next, put your hands out in front of you as if to push away something you didn't want and say, "I resist the notion of my goal not being achieved. I push away the consequences."

Now raise your hands above your head and pray, "Father, with open arms of gratitude, and according to your promises, I receive this goal you have placed within me. I celebrate it to see it."

Then pull your hands down towards your heart as if pulling fruit off of a tree. Then say, "I receive, Lord. I believe—so be it."

Step Five – Boundaries
(Analyze Starting Point / Define Completion / Boundaries)

"The boundary lines have fallen for me in the pleasant places; surely I have a delightful inheritance"
(Psalm 16:6)

Analyze Starting Point

For each of your goals, write down your current starting position. For instance, if your goal is to have $1 million dollars cash by age 55, write down how much cash you have now. If you are trying to achieve a certain weight, write down your current weight.

Where are you currently?

_____

Now clearly define your goal as completed:

_____

Step Six – Time
(Set a Deadline / Set a Starting Date / The Stopwatch)

"For everything there is a season, a time for every activity under Heaven"
(Eccl 3:1)

Now write down a start date for your primary goal.

I will begin _____
(My goal)

on _____.
(My start date)

Now write down a deadline. Use a future date in the present tense, Example: "I weigh __X__ pounds on June 1, 2014."

_____
(My goal)

_____.
(My completion date)

Now read the goal and the start date and deadline aloud so you hear it for yourself.

www.MaximumDreamAchievement.com

Step Seven – Survey
(List Obstacles / Identify Opportunities / Survey Terrain)

"Look the land over, see what it is like"
(Numbers 13:17-20)

List five opportunities that you can think of that currently align with your goal on which you can capitalize:

1. _____
2. _____
3. _____
4. _____
5. _____

Circle the best opportunity for you at this time and say out loud, "I will seize this opportunity now."

List the three biggest obstacles or fears that could hold you back from obtaining your goal.

1. _____
2. _____
3. _____

Now declare out loud that these obstacles are small, insignificant, and have no power over your destiny.

www.MaximumDreamAchievement.com

Step Eight – Information
(Identify Information / List Resources / Research)

"Wisdom is supreme; therefore get wisdom"
(Prov 4:7)

Make a list of information that you will need to gather. What books will you need to read, or courses will you have to take?

Ask those who have a measure of success in doing you are attempting to do to share with you their sources of wisdom.

Use the Internet to identify those who have accomplished what you are planning to do. Check to see if they have written books or hold seminars. Maybe they have a mentorship or coaching program.

Make a list of at least five resources that you are going to tap into to do your research. If you can come up with 10 or 20 that's great. But start with at least five. Dedicate at least 20 minutes per day to research your target area. Make your list:

1. _____
2. _____
3. _____
4. _____
5. _____
6. _____
7. _____
8. _____
9. _____
10. _____
11. _____
12. _____
13. _____
14. _____
15. _____

16._____
17._____
18._____
19._____
20._____

www.MaximumDreamAchievement.com

Step Nine – Advocates
(Identify Helpers / Identify Those to Avoid / Advocacy)

"But the advocate the Holy Spirit, whom the Father will send in my name, will teach you all things…"
(John 14:26)

Make a list of your three closest advocates:

1. _____
2. _____
3. _____

Contact each of them in the next 48 hours and tell them that you are grateful that they are in the inner-inner circle.

Ask if you may share your goals and dreams with them and invite them to share theirs with you.

Next, list the twelve people with whom you are "in relationship." Contact your twelve over the next seven days and let them know how important they are to you; and thank them for being your "advocate." Let them know that you are an "advocate" for them. Ask if you may share your dreams and goals with them and invite them to share theirs with you.

See if there is a match in your list of twelve with their twelve, and ask if they feel that their advocates might be a match for yours. Finally, make a written commitment to avoid negative people and reduce your contact with news media.

1. _____
2. _____
3. _____
4. _____
5. _____
6. _____

7. _____
8. _____
9. _____
10. _____
11. _____
12. _____

Step Ten – Plan
(Make a Plan / Take Action / Activation)

"Therefore go"
(Matt 28:19)

In your goals journal, make a simple 10 bullet point plan of action for how you are going to accomplish your goal.

1. _____
2. _____
3. _____
4. _____
5. _____
6. _____
7. _____
8. _____
9. _____
10. _____

Next, list the first simple step you are going to take in the next 48 hours to *activate* your goal. Then take that action and say to yourself, "Activation has begun…so be it."

www.MaximumDreamAchievement.com

Action Plan

Make a one-year goal and put it into a plan of action timeline exercise like I have done with my book example.

A) 1-3 Days	B) 3-10 Days	C) 10-30 Days	D) 30-90 Days	E) 3 mos–1 yr
_____ _____ _____	_____ _____ _____	_____ _____ _____	_____ _____ _____	_____ _____ _____
_____ _____ _____	_____ _____ _____	_____ _____ _____	_____ _____ _____	_____ _____ _____
_____ _____ _____	_____ _____ _____	_____ _____ _____	_____ _____ _____	_____ _____ _____
_____ _____ _____	_____ _____ _____	_____ _____ _____	_____ _____ _____	_____ _____ _____

Step Eleven – Consume
(Visualize / Emotionalize / Internalize)

"I was blind but now I see"
(John 9:25)

Perhaps you are familiar with NLP, which stands for Neuro-linguistic Programming. Science has determined that our words and our physical bodies work in sync with each other. That's another good reason for us to guard our speech, isn't it?

At this point, we want to use a simple NLP technique, one that professional athletes and other high-performance individuals use to solidify their goals. This process is called "anchoring."

So, with your written goal in front of you, read it aloud. Put your hand on your head, close your eyes, and say, "___(Your goal)_____ – so shall it be."

Then put your hand on your heart and repeat your goal and the words – "so shall it be."

Then put your hand on your stomach and repeat the goal and again finish with "so shall it be."

At this point you have anchored yourself to your goal and have deemed it "done." Repeat this process each day. It only takes a few minutes and it will change your life.

Step Twelve – Power
(Persistence / Patience / Prayer)

"Your Kingdom come, your will be done"
(Matthew 6:10)

Write your goal now as accomplished. Draw a circle around it. Put your finger on it and say aloud, "I commit to this purpose and will persist until it appears."

Now close your eyes and say, "I will peacefully and patiently enjoy the process.

Now say to yourself, "God, grant me this goal as an inheritance of the dream that you planted inside of me. Thank you. In Jesus' name, Amen."

www.MaximumDreamAchievement.com

APPENDIX A:

How to Be Born Again

You May Need a Heart Transplant

When I (Eddie) was a young traveling evangelist, in December 1967 on a cold Sunday night, I had finished the crusade service, enjoyed dinner, and was snuggled warmly in my motel bed, watching the late evening news, when I heard a startling announcement. South African surgeon (and preacher's son) Dr. Christiaan Barnard had performed the world's first human heart transplant. He'd placed the heart of Denise Darvall, a woman in her mid-20s, fatally injured in an automobile accident, inside the chest of fifty-five-year-old diabetic Louis Washkansky, who had incurable heart disease. The new heart was actually beating on its own! That, my friend, was amazing.

When the interviewer asked Dr. Barnard why he had decided to perform such a risky operation, his answer caused me to bolt upright in bed: "One look at Mr. Washkansky and I knew he couldn't live with that old heart." Tears immediately flooded my eyes as I realized that I too couldn't have lived with my old heart. If you've never had one, you also need a heart transplant. Not a physical heart transplant, but a spiritual one.

The Word of God tells us that *"the heart is deceitful above all things and desperately wicked"* (Jeremiah 17:9). It says that *"all (of us) have sinned, and come short of the glory of God"* (Romans 3:23). This means that we all have "spiritual heart disease that is always fatal, for *"the wages of sin is death"* (Romans 6:23). This means spiritual death, separation from God, *in this life and for eternity.*

We're beyond the need of a spiritual heart massage--only a new heart will do. *Everyone needs a new heart.*

Good news! God loves you and wants you to experience peace, and abundant eternal life. Today he says to you, *"A new heart also will I give you ... and I will take away the stony heart out of your flesh"* (Ezek. 36:26). The heavenly Father wants to perform the transplant you need. You cannot pay for the operation because Jesus Christ has already paid the price when He died for your sins and mine on the cross. Today you can have a new heart, a clean heart, a pure heart by doing just as David, the psalmist did. He asked God for it: *"Create in me a clean heart, O God"* (Ps. 51:10). And guess what—the Lord did!

God didn't create us as robots that would automatically obey and serve him. He created us in his own image and gave us freedom to choose—yes, even freedom to choose Him.

Like the first man and woman, Adam and Eve, chose their own way in the Garden of Eden and sinned against God, we too have chosen to disobey God and go our own way. The result is: our sin separates us from God.

Worse still—as hard as we may try, and regardless of our good intentions, there is no way for us to be reconciled to God apart from Jesus Christ. Only Christ, his cross, and His resurrection can reconnect us to God.

Jesus died on the cross and arose from the grave three days later in order to pay the penalty for our sin and bridge the gap between God and us.

Here is the solution:
1. Recognize and admit that you've sinned against God.
2. Acknowledge that you need a Savior, for you cannot save yourself.
3. Repent by turning from your sins.

4. Believe in your heart that Jesus died for you and three days later the heavenly Father raised Him from the dead—He is alive.
5. Now trust Jesus Christ as your personal Lord and Savior by inviting Him to live in your heart through his Holy Spirit.

Are you ready? Good!

Right now, right where you are, turn to God and say,

> *"Dear God, I know that I have sinned against you. I am a sinner. I need your forgiveness. I need a new, clean heart. I am turning from my sins. Forgive and cleanse me. I trust you as my Savior and give my life to you. Come into my heart today, Risen Christ, and be Lord of my life. I choose to follow you. Thank you for the new life you've given me. Thank you for my new, clean heart. In Jesus' name I pray. Amen"*

Did you sincerely turn to Christ? Did you invite Him into your life? Then congratulations! He has washed away your sins and lives in you! This is salvation, or what the Scripture calls being born again. It is a supernatural work of God's Spirit who lives in you now.

This is the only cure for spiritual heart trouble. Now, with Jesus Christ as your Savior and with the new heart He has given you, you have everlasting life! Now you can relate to Him on a brand-new level. He is your Father, and you are His child. Best of all, when you take your last breath and pass from this physical body, you'll be present with God in heaven and will live with Him forever!

> *"Blessed are the pure in heart: for they shall see God"*
> (Matthew 5:8)

"The Lord seeth not as man seeth; for man looketh on the outward appearance, but the Lord looketh on the heart" (1 Sam. 16:7).

Here are some helpful steps you can take to develop and deepen your new relationship with God.

1. Get to know God by reading your Bible each day. I suggest you start with the New Testament book of Philippians. You will find it easy to read and to apply to your daily life. Then read the Gospel of John.
2. Converse with God continually through prayer. Talk to him. He is your Father now. Tell him how you feel and what you want.
3. When you sin, don't let your sins pile up and rob you of your joy. Make a practice of confess and repent of your sins quickly.
4. Above all, listen to him. He will speak to your heart through his Holy Spirit.
5. Attend a good Bible-teaching church where you can worship and serve God and fellowship with other believers.
6. Ask the pastor to baptize you, as Jesus has commanded each of us. Water baptism is a symbol of your putting off your old life and putting on your new life in Christ. It is a picture of a burial and resurrection.
7. Share your new life with others. Invite them to do as you have done, so they can experience God's peace and live forever with Him.

www.MaximumDreamAchievement.com

About the Authors

Kenn Renner is a national speaker, author, investor, and entrepreneur. He has closed over $250 million in sales as a top producing real estate broker. He created the #1 ranked YouTube channel for real estate nationwide. He has produced a multitude of educational and motivational programs including seminars, television shows, music CDs, books, DVDs, video & audio programs. Kenn resides in Austin, TX with his wife Michele and his children Justin, Christine, and Julia. He enjoys songwriting, travel, golf, and wintersports. (More at: www.BuyAustin.com)

Products & Services
(All products available at www.KennRenner.com)

Home Buying Secrets Revealed 
Home Buying Secrets Revealed will give you the opportunity to learn key tips and strategies from an industry expert who has specialized in helping home buyers for the past 30 years.
www.HomeBuyingSecretsRevealed.com

Power Goals (also available in audio book) 
The preliminary version of Maximum Dream Achievement, Power Goals takes you through twelve steps that will take you from anywhere you are at to where you want to go.
www.PowerGoalsBook.com

Video Quick Start Guide 
78% of sellers want their Realtor to have an online video presence yet only 12% of them have a YouTube channel. The Video Quick Start Guide will show you how to leverage the power of video in your real estate business.
www.VideoQuickStartGuide.com (Free download!)

BuyAustin.Com
BuyAustin.com is the premiere Ausitn, TX real estate website featuring in-depth knowledge and resources for those seeking to buy, sell or invest. Call Kenn today at 512-423-5626

www.MaximumDreamAchievement.com

#1 YouTube Channel for Real Estate
Kenn Renner has the #1 Real Estate YouTube channel in the world with 11 million views, 700 videos, and 9000 subscribers. Let him put his online video marketing to work on your home today! www.YouTube.Com/RennerRealty

Eddie Smith, a bestselling author of too many books to mention here and internationally known conference speaker, is a Christian minister who is founder and president of the U.S. Prayer Center. He has written and co-written many books with his wife Alice Smith and others.

In more than 50 years in ministry Eddie has served as an evangelist, a pastor, and on many committees including the National Prayer Committee, the U.S. Lausanne Committee, the Mission America Coalition executive team, and others.

In the business realm Eddie is a motivational speaker; a marketing coach, a writing coach, and a life coach. He's a ghostwriter, copywriter, editor and publisher.

Ministry site: www.USPrayerCenter.org

Ministry resources site: www.PrayerBookstore.com and www.TeachMeToPray.com

Other resources: www.NuWayCommunications.com and www.Pastoral-Counseling.com

How can I serve you? Call me today at 281-830-8724

Made in the USA
Columbia, SC
01 June 2021